John Edward Gray

Synopsis of the Species of Whales and Dolphins in the

Collection of the British Museum

John Edward Gray

Synopsis of the Species of Whales and Dolphins in the Collection of the British Museum

ISBN/EAN: 9783337329082

Printed in Europe, USA, Canada, Australia, Japan

Cover: Foto ©ninafisch / pixelio.de

More available books at **www.hansebooks.com**

SYNOPSIS OF THE SPECIES

OF

WHALES AND DOLPHINS

IN THE

COLLECTION OF THE BRITISH MUSEUM.

(ILLUSTRATED WITH 37 PLATES, BY THE LATE WILLIAM WING.)

BY

JOHN EDWARD GRAY, Ph.D., F.R.S., V.P.Z.S., F.L.S., ETC.,
KEEPER OF THE ZOOLOGICAL COLLECTIONS IN THE BRITISH MUSEUM.

LONDON:
BERNARD QUARITCH, 15 PICCADILLY.
MDCCCLXVIII.

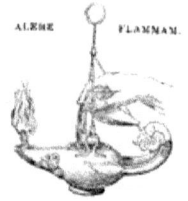

PRINTED BY TAYLOR AND FRANCIS,
RED LION COURT, FLEET STREET.

SYNOPSIS

OF THE

SPECIES OF WHALES AND DOLPHINS.

CETACEA.

Teeth all similar, conical, sometimes not developed. Palate often furnished with transverse plates of baleen or whalebone. Body fish-shaped, smooth, bald. Limbs clawless; fore limbs fin-shaped; hinder united, forming a forked horizontal fin. Nostrils enlarged into blowers. Teats two, inguinal. Carnivorous.

Section I. **MYSTICETE**, *Gray, Cat. Seals & Whales B. M.* 62, 68.
(*Mystacocete* or *Balænoidea*, Flower, Trans. Z. S. vi. 110.)

Head large, depressed. Teeth rudimentary; they never cut the gums. Palate with transverse, fringed, horny plates of baleen. Nostrils separate, longitudinal. Gullet very contracted. Tympanic bones simple, large, cochleate, attached to an expanded periotic bone, which forms part of the skull.

Suborder I. **BALÆNOIDEA**.

Belly smooth. Head very large. Baleen elongate. Dorsal fin none.

Family I. BALÆNIDÆ, *Gray, Cat. Seals & Whales B. M.* 64, 75; *Lilljeborg, N. Acta Upsal.* 1867, vi.

Dorsal fin none. Belly smooth. Baleen elongate, slender. Vertebræ of the neck anchylosed. Pectoral fin broad, truncated at the end; fingers five. Tympanic bones rhombic; maxillary bones narrow.

I. *Baleen thin, polished, with a thick enamel on each side, and a fine elongate slender fringe.*

1. BALÆNA, *Gray, l. c.* 79; *Lilljeborg, N. Acta Upsal.* vi. 1867.

First rib slender, narrow, and undivided at the vertebral end. Tympanic bones square; aperture nearly as long as the bone. The upper and lower lateral processes of the atlas vertebra obliquely truncated.

1. **Balæna mysticetus** (T. 1. f. 1, baleen), *Linn.*; *Gray, l. c.* 81, figs. 1, 2, 4, 5. *Hab.* North Sea.

2. **Balæna marginata** (T. 1. f. 1, baleen), *Gray l. c.* 90. *Hab.* Western Australia: a very small species.

II. *Baleen thick, not polished, with a thin enamel coat on each side, and a coarse thick fringe.*

II. EUBALÆNA, *Gray, l. c.* 91; *Lilljeborg, N. Acta Upsal.* vi. 1867.

First rib broad at the vertebral end. Tympanic bone square; aperture nearly as long as the bone.

1. **Eubalæna australis**, *Gray, l. c.* 91, fig. 6. Balæna australis, *Cuv. Oss. Foss.* v. t. 25-27. (B. capensis, T. 1. f. 3, baleen). *Hab.* Cape of Good Hope.

2. **Eubalæna Sieboldii** (T. 1. f. 2, baleen), *Gray, l. c.* 96. (Balæna japonica, *Gray*, T. 1. f. 2, baleen.) B. australis, *Temm. F. Japon.* t. 28, 29. *Hab.* Japan.

See *E. cisarctica*, Cope, Journ. Acad. N. S. Philad. 1865, p. 168.

III. HUNTERIUS, *Gray, l. c.* 78, 98; *Lilljeborg, N. Acta Upsal.* vi. 1867.

First rib broad, with a doublehead at the vertebral end. Tympanic bones square; aperture nearly as long as the bone.

1. **Hunterius Temminckii**, *Gray, l. c.* 98, fig. 8. Balæna australis, *Temm. F. Japon.* t. 28, 29. *Hab.* Cape of Good Hope.

2. **Hunterius Swedenborgii**, *Lilljeborg, N. Acta A. Sci. Upsal.* vi. (1867,) 35, t. 9, 10, 11 (skeleton). *Hab.* North Sea, Sweden (subfossil).

See *Hunterius Biscayensis* (*Balæna Biscayensis*, Gray, l. c. 89). *Hab.* North Atlantic. Mus. Copenhagen, jun.

IV. CAPEREA, *Gray, l. c.* 78, 101; *Lilljeborg, N. Acta Upsal.* vi. 1867.

First rib ——. Baleen ——? Tympanic bones irregular, rhombic; aperture irregular, much contracted at the upper end; the wide part not half the length of the bone. "Cervical vertebræ all united. First rib single at the upper, and very broad at the lower end. Bladebone (acromion) rudimentary. Coracoid process none."—*Lilljeborg*.

1. **Caperea antipodarum**, *Gray, l. c.* 101, fig. 9. *Balæna antipodarum*, *Gray, Dieffenbach*, t. 1. *Hab.* New Zealand. Skeleton, Mus. Paris.

V. MACLEAYIUS, *Gray, l. c.* 103, 37.

First rib ——. Baleen ——? The upper and lateral process of the atlas vertebra broad and truncated.

1. **Macleayius australiensis**, *Gray, l. c.* 105 (figs. 10, 11), 374 (figs. 74, 75). *Hab.* Australian Seas.

Suborder II. BALÆNOPTEROIDEA.

(*Balænopteridæ*, Gray, l. c. 61, 106.)

Dorsal fin distinct. Belly longitudinally plaited. Baleen short, broad. Maxillary bones broad. Pectoral fin lanceolate; fingers four. Vertebræ of the neck free. Tympanic bones oblong or ovate.

Family II. MEGAPTERIDÆ.
(*Megapterina*, Gray, l. c. 113.)

Dorsal fin low, broad. Pectoral fin very long, with four very long fingers of many phalanges. Vertebræ fifty or sixty; cervical vertebræ often anchylosed. Lateral processes of the axis tardily ossified. Neural canal large, high, triangular. Ribs fourteen or fifteen.

I. MEGAPTERA, *Gray, l. c.* 113, 117; *Lilljeborg, N. Acta Upsal.* 1867, vi. Hump-backed Whale.

Bladebone without acromion or coracoid process. Body of cervical vertebræ subcircular.

1. **Megaptera longimana**, *Gray, l. c.* 119 (fig.), 373. M. Boops (Tab. 30, baleen and jaws with rudimentary teeth; T. 33. f. 12, vertebra). *Hab.* North Sea.

2. **Megaptera Novæ-Zelandiæ**, *Gray, l. c.* 128. fig.

II. POESCOPIA, *Gray, l. c.* 113.

Bladebone with small coracoid process. Body of cervical vertebræ nearly square.

1. **Poescopia Lalandii**, *Gray, l. c.* 126 (fig.), 373 (Tab. 33. f. 3, 4, vertebræ, from Cuvier). *Hab.* Cape of Good Hope.

III. ESCHRICHTIUS, *Gray, l. c.* 113, 131; *Lilljeborg, N. Acta Upsal.* vi. 12, 1867.

Bladebone with large coracoid process. Body of cervical vertebræ separate, small, roundish-oblong. The neural canal very broad and high.

1. **Eschrichtius robustus**, *Gray, l. c.* 133 (fig.), 373. *Lilljeborg, N. Acta Upsal.* 1867, vi. 16, t. 1–8. *Hab.* North Sea, coast of Devonshire, Sweden.

Family III. PHYSALINIDÆ.
(*Physalina*, Gray, l. c. 114, 134.)

Dorsal fin high, erect, compressed, falcate, about three-fourths the entire length from the nose. Pectoral fin moderate, with four short fingers, of four or six phalanges. Vertebræ 55 or 64. Cervical vertebræ not anchylosed. Neural canal oblong, transverse.

* *Vertebræ 60 or 64; first rib single-headed.*

I. BENEDENIA, *Gray, l. c.* 114, 135.

Rostrum of skull narrow, attenuated, with straight slanting edges. Second cervical vertebra with two short truncated lateral processes. The first rib single-headed.

1. **Benedenia Knoxii**, *Gray, l. c.* 138, figs. 24–26. *B. Boops*, Tab. 32. f. 1, 2 (cervical vertebræ). *Hab.* North Sea, coast of Wales.

II. PHYSALUS, *Gray, l. c.* 114, 139; *Lilljeborg, N. Acta Upsal.* 1867, p. 72.

Rostrum of the skull narrow, attenuated, with straight sloping sides. Second cervical vertebra with a broad lateral process, with a large perforation at the base. First rib single-headed. Sternum trifoliate, with a long slender hinder process.

† *Lateral rings of the second cervical vertebra as long as the diameter of the body of the vertebra.* Gray, l. c. 37.

1. **Physalus antiquorum** (Tab. 1. f. 6, baleen; T. 3. f. 5, 6, cervical vertebræ), *Gray, l. c.* 144 (figs. 29–32), 374. Ribs 14.14. *Hab.* North Sea, Greenland, Hampshire, &c.

2. **Physalus Duguldii**, *Gray, l. c.* 158 (figs 33–35). Ribs 15.15. *Hab.* North Sea, Orkneys.

†† *The lateral rings of the cervical vertebræ shorter than the diameter of the body of the vertebræ.* Gray, l. c. 374.

3. **Physalus patachonicus**, *Gray, l. c.* 374 (figs. 76–80). *Hab.* River Plata.

III. CUVIERIUS, *Gray, l. c.* 114, 164.

Rostrum of the skull broad, the outer side curved, especially in front. The second cervical vertebra with two short thick lateral processes. First rib single-headed. Sternum oblong-ovate, transverse.

1. **Cuvierius Sibbaldii**, *Gray, l. c.* 380. C. latirostris, *Gray, l. c.* 165. Physalus Sibbaldii, *Gray, l. c.* 160 (fig. 36), 380. Balænoptera Sibbaldii (T. 33. f. 5, 6, vertebræ). Balænoptera Carolinæ, *Malm, Moscg. Illust.* t. 14. *Hab.* North Sea. Mus. Hull.

** *Vertebræ 55. First and second ribs double-headed. Second cervical vertebra with a broad lateral process perforated at the base. Lower jaw compressed, with distinct coronoid process.* Sibbaldius, *Gray, l. c.* 114, 169.

IV. RUDOLPHIUS, *Gray, l. c.* 170, 1865. Sibbaldius, *Lilljeborg, Nova Acta, Upsal.* vi. 1867.

Dorsal fin compressed, falcate, two-thirds of the entire length from the nose. Ribs 13. 13; first rib short, dilated at the sternal end. Sternum elongate, not narrow at posterior lobe.

1. **Rudolphius laticeps.** Sibbaldius laticeps, *Gray, l. c.* 170, figs. 37, 38. *Hab.* North Sea.

V. SIBBALDIUS, *Gray, l. c.* 175, 1865. Flowerius, *Lilljeborg, N. Acta Upsal.* vi. 1867.

Dorsal fin very small, far behind, and placed on a thick prominence. Ribs 14. 14; first short, sternal end very broad and deeply notched. Sternum with a broad short hinder lobe.

1. **Sibbaldius borealis**, *Gray, l. c.* 175, fig. 39. Flowerius gigas, *Lilljeborg, N. Acta Upsal.* vi. 1867. *Hab.* North Sea.

2. **Sibbaldius Schlegellii**, *Gray, l. c.* 178, figs. 40–48. *Hab.* Java.

3. **Sibbaldius? antarcticus**, *Gray, l. c.* 381, fig. 87. *Hab.* Buenos Ayres.

Family IV. BALÆNOPTERIDÆ.
(*Balænopterina*, *Gray, l. c.* 114. *Balænoptera*, *Gray, l. c.* 114; *Lilljeborg*, vi.)

Dorsal fin high, erect, compressed, about two-thirds of the entire length from the nose. Pectoral fin moderate, with four short fingers. Vertebræ 50; cervical vertebræ sometimes anchylosed. Neural canal broad, trigonal. Ribs 11. 11. The second cervical vertebra with a broad lateral expansion perforated at the base. First rib single-headed. Lower jaw with a conical coronoid process.

I. BALÆNOPTERA, *Gray, l. c.* 114.

The lower lateral processes of the third to the seventh cervical vertebræ with an angular projection on the lower edges. Fabricia, *Gray, l. c.* 382.

1. **Balænoptera rostrata** (T. 1. f. 5, baleen; T. 2, skull; T. 32. f. 3, 4, cervical vertebræ), *Gray, l. c.* 188, figs. 49–53. *Hab.* North Sea.

II. SWINHOIA, *Gray, l. c.* 382.

The lower lateral processes of the third to the sixth cervical vertebræ slender, regularly curved, without any prominent angle on the lower edge.

1. **Swinhoia chinensis.** Balænoptera Swinhoei, *Gray, l. c.* 382, figs. 88–93. *Hab.* Formosa.

Section II. **DENTICETE**, *Gray, l. c.* 62, 194.
(*Odontoceti* or *Delphinoidea*, Flower, *l. c.* 111.)

Teeth well developed in one or both jaws, sometimes deciduous. Palate without baleen. Head large or moderate, compressed. Tympanic bones two, dissimilar, separate, becoming united, sunk in a cavity in the base of the skull. Gullet large.

The suborders in the section have certain relations to each other in two parallel series:—

Teeth only in the lower jaw. Cervical vertebræ often united	A. Nostrils separate, elongated.	B. Nostrils united, transverse.
Teeth only in the lower jaw. Cervical vertebræ often united	Physeteroidea	Ziphioidea
Teeth well developed in both jaws. Jaws beaked	Susuoidea	Delphinoidea

Suborder III. **PHYSETEROIDEA**, *Gray, l. c.* 195.

Head blunt. Nostrils longitudinal, parallel or diverging, each covered with a valve, the right often obliterated. Teeth only in the lower jaw, fitting into holes in the gums of the upper one.

Family V. CATODONTIDÆ.
(*Catodontina*, Gray, *l. c.* 386, 387).

Head compressed, truncated in front, very large. Blowers separate, linear, in front of the upper part of the head. Mouth inferior, linear. Pectoral fin short, broad, truncate. Dorsal hump rounded. Skull elongate. Crown concave, surrounded by a high perpendicular wall formed by the doubled-up maxilla and occipital bones. Upper jaw toothless.

I. CATODON, *Gray, l. c.* 196, 386, 387.

The atlas vertebra transverse, nearly twice as broad as high; the central canal subtrigonal, narrow below.

1. **Catodon macrocephalus**, *Gray, l. c.* 196, f. 54, 202, 387. *Hab.* Tropical seas, accidentally in the temperate ones. Mr. Flower (Trans. Zool. Soc. vi.) considers *C. australis*, Gray, *l. c.* 206, fig. 55, the same species.

II. MEGANEURON, *Gray, l. c.* 386, 387.

The atlas vertebra subcircular, rather broader than high. The central canal subcircular, in the middle of the body, widened above.

1. **Meganeuron Krefftii**, *Gray*, P. Z. S. 1865, p. 440; *l. c.* 388, figs. 94–97. *Hab.* Australian Seas.

Family VI. PHYSETERIDÆ.
(*Physeterina*, Gray, *l. c.* 386, 390.)

Head depressed, rounded in front. Blowers linear (the one on the left side often only open), at the back of the forehead. Mouth small, inferior, rounded. Dorsal fin compressed, falcate. Pectoral fin elongate, falcate. Skull short; crown concave; hinder part of the wall formed by the maxillaries, and divided, as it were, into two subequal parts by a central bony ridge, which is more or less twisted towards the right side. Upper jaw toothless.

1. PHYSETER, *Gray, l. c.* 196, 211, 386.

Head large, rather depressed in front. Skull ——?

1. **Physeter tursio**, *Linn*; *Gray, l. c.* 212. *Hab.* North Sea, Scotland, *Sibbald*, 1687. Length 52 or 53 feet.

II. KOGIA, *Gray, l. c.* 196, 215, 386, 391.

Head moderate, blunt, and high in front; left blower only open. Skull short and broad; the septum that divides the crown of the skull very sinuous, folded so as to form a funnel-shaped cavity.

1. **Kogia breviceps**, *Gray, l. c.* 217, 391. *Hab.* Cape of Good Hope. Perhaps the next is the same species.

2. **Kogia Macleayii**, *Gray, l. c.* 391. Physeter simus, *Owen, Trans. Zool. Soc.* vi. 30, t. 10, 11, 12, 13, 2 (not skeleton, t. 11. f. 2). *Hab.* Australia, India. Length 10 feet, young.

The difference between *Kogia* and *Euphysetes* does not depend on the sex of the animals. Mr. Krefft described a male, and Professor Owen a female, specimen; the latter mistook the two drawings of the same specimen for the two sexes, deceived by certain additions surreptitiously made to Mr. Elliot's drawings; but these additions, especially the penis, is not represented on the Plates, and the artist (Mr. Willis) says he received no directions to leave out any part of the drawing, and accurately copied them. The measurements given in the paper do not agree with those in Mr. Elliot's notes made from the living animal, and the references to them would have prevented all this confusion.

III. EUPHYSETES, *Gray, l. c.* 196, 215, 386, 392.

Head moderate, blunt, and high in front. Skull short and broad. The septum that divides the cavity of the crown of the skull simple, longitudinal, only slightly curved.

1. **Euphysetes Grayii**, *MacLeay*; *Gray, l. c.* 218, 392. Physeter simus, *Owen, Trans. Zool. Soc.* vi. t. 11. f. 2 (skeleton only). *Hab.* Australia.

Suborder IV. SUSUOIDEA.

Head beaked. Nostrils longitudinal, each covered with a valve (the right often obliterated). Teeth in upper and lower jaws, compressed. Crown of skull covered with a bony arch.

Family VII. PLATANISTIDÆ, *Gray, l. c.* 52, 220.

Head long-beaked. Jaws slender, compressed. Teeth in both jaws, compressed. Skull—crown covered with the converging arch and reflexed edges of the maxillaries.

I. PLATANISTA, *Gray, l. c.* 221.

1. **Platanista gangetica**, *Gray, l. c.* 223. *Hab.* India, Ganges.

2. **Platanista Indi**, *Gray, l. c.* 224. *Hab.* India, Indus.

Suborder V. DELPHINOIDEA.

Nostrils two, united into a single central transverse or crescentic blower on the back of the crown. Teeth in both jaws, permanent. Pectoral fin lanceolate. Head beaked. Dorsal fin falcate or wanting. Skull—maxillary bone spread out over the orbit.

Family VIII. INIIDÆ, *Gray, l. c.* 62, 226.

Fluviatile. Head beaked; beak bristly. Teeth in the jaws rugulose, crowns with an internal lobe; permanent. Back keeled behind, without any dorsal fin. Skull—jaw compressed; symphysis of lower jaw elongate, overlooking the front of the blower. Mr. Flower places this genus with *Platanistidæ*.

I. INIA, *Gray, l. c.* 226; *Flower, l. c.* 1.

1. **Inia Geoffroyii**, *Gray, l. c.* 226, 393; *Flower, Trans. Zool. Soc.* vi. 87, t. 25, 26, 27 (skeleton). D. amazonicus, *Spix*. *Hab.* Brazil, River Amazons.

Family IX. DELPHINIDÆ, *Gray, l. c.* 230, 393.

Head beaked. Teeth in both jaws, conical or compressed, permanent, without any internal lobe, occupying nearly the whole length of the jaws. Back rounded, with a falcate dorsal fin, rarely absent. Skull with the maxilla expanded over the orbit, and more or less turned up on the edges.

1. *Pectoral fin elongate, falcate (except in Sotalia), acute at the end; hand as long as the arm-bones; forearm-bones close together, only separated by a straight line. Carpal bones moderate, 5 or 7.*

Tribe I. STENONINA.

Head beaked. Beak of the skull elongate, slender, compressed. Nasal triangle short. Symphysis of the lower jaw elongate. Gray, P. Z. S. 1866, p. 212.

I. PONTOPORIA, Gray, l. c. 230, 231, 393, 1846.
(Stenodelphis, Gervais, 1847.)

Beak of the skull high, compressed. Symphysis of the lower jaw very long. Dorsal fin ——? Blowhole ——?

1. **Pontoporia Blainvillii** (T. 29, skull), Gray, l. c. 231; Flower, Trans. Zool. Soc. vi. 106, t. 18 (skull). *Hab.* South Atlantic, Monte Video.

II. STENO, Gray, l. c. 230, 232, 393, 394.

Beak of the skull compressed, higher than broad. Symphysis of the lower jaw long. Marine and fluviatile.

a. *Skull large, solid, the beak compressed, high. Teeth large, conical, about two in an inch of the length of the margin of the jaw.*

1. **Steno frontatus**, Gray, l. c. 233. n. 3. Beak of the skull short; the front part thick, high, and blunt. Teeth 24. 2 b, large, two in an inch. *Hab.* Indian Ocean.

2. **Steno compressus** (T. 27), Gray, l. c. 233. n. 4. Beak of the skull elongate, compressed, attenuated in front. Teeth 26. 26, large, two in an inch (Zool. E. & T. t. 27). *Hab.* South Sea.

Steno rostratus appears to belong to this section.

b. *Skull small, rather spongy. Teeth small, slender, attenuated, about four or five in an inch of the length of the margin of the jaw.*

* *Beak of the skull elongate, compressed, much attenuated and acute in front. Teeth four in an inch.* Sousa.

3. **Steno capensis**, Gray, l. c. 394. n. 4*. *Hab.* Cape of Good Hope.

4. **Steno lentiginosus**, Gray, l. c. 394. n. 4**; Owen, Trans. Zool. Soc. vi. t. 5. f. 2, 3. *Hab.* India (W. Elliot). Skull, B. M.

The skull of *Steno roseiventris*, according to the figure, appears to belong to this section of the genus.

** *Beak of the skull short, compressed, much attenuated and acute in front. Teeth five in an inch.* Tucuxa.

5. **Steno tucuxi**, Gray, l. c. 237, 394. *Hab.* Brazil, River Amazons, 1500 miles from the sea (Bates).

See also S. *fluviatilis* and S. *pallidus*, Gray, l. c. 237; same locality, if distinct.

*** *Beak of the skull elongate, rather depressed, broad, slightly compressed on the sides. Teeth small, five in an inch.* Stenella.

6. **Steno attenuatus** (T. 28), Gray, l. c. 235, 394. The beak of the skull flattened (Zool. E. & T. t. 28). *Hab.* India.

This last section is nearly intermediate between *Steno* and *Clymenia*.

Steno fuscus (T. 26. f. 1), only known from a fœtus in spirits.

Tribe II. DELPHININA.

Head beaked. Beak of the skull elongate, depressed, broad, shelving on the sides. Nasal triangle short. Symphysis of the lower jaw short, sloping.

a. *Palate with a deep groove on each side behind.*

I. DELPHINUS, Gray, l. c. 230, 393.

Beak elongate. Dorsal fin distinct. Teeth small, slender, five or six in an inch. (Fœtus and tongue figured, T. 26. f. 2)

* *Beak of skull twice as long as the brain-case. Teeth $\frac{50}{50}$ or $\frac{54}{54}$.*

1. **Delphinus longirostris**, Gray, l. c. 211. n. 2. *Hab.* Southern Ocean, Cape of Good Hope, Japan, Malabar.

** *Beak of skull once and a half the length of the brain-case. Teeth $\frac{43}{46}$ to $\frac{50}{50}$.*

2. **Delphinus delphis**, Gray, l. c. 212. n. 3, 395. Black, sides grey, beneath white. *Hab.* North Sea, North Atlantic, Mediterranean.

3. **Delphinus Moorei**, Gray, l. c. 396, fig. 99. *Hab.* South Atlantic.

4. **Delphinus major**, Gray, l. c. 396. *Hab.* ——?

5. **Delphinus Walkeri**, Gray, l. c. 397, fig. 100. *Hab.* South Atlantic.

6. **Delphinus Janira** (T. 23), Gray, l. c. 245, 398; Zool. E. & T. t. 23. *Hab.* Newfoundland.

7. **Delphinus pomeegra**, Owen, Trans. Zool. Soc. vi. t. 6. f. 3, t. 8. *Hab.* India (W. Elliot). Skull, B. M.

8. **Delphinus Forsteri** (T. 24), copied from Forster's drawing; the skull not known.

b. *Palate flat behind, without any lateral grooves.*

II. CLYMENIA.

Clymene, Gray, *l. c.* 249; P. Z. S. 1864, p. 237, 1866, p. 214.

Beak of skull elongate, depressed. Teeth small, slender. Nasal triangle moderate. Dorsal fin distinct. Pectoral fin falcate; hand larger than the forearm-bones. Skull elongate, slender; brain-case spherical; beak slender, elongate, longer than the brain-case; intermaxillaries convex. Teeth small, slender, five or six in an inch. The symphysis of the lower jaw short. The blowers are moderate.

* *Beak of the skull twice as long as the brain-case. Teeth five in an inch.* Micropia.

1. **Clymenia stenorhyncha,** *Gray*, P. Z. S. 1866, p. 214. Delphinus stenorhynchus, Gray, *l. c.* 396. n. 1*. D. microps, Gray, *l. c.* 240.

** *Beak of the skull once and three-quarters the length of the brain-cavity. Teeth six in an inch.* Euphrosyne.

2. **Clymenia microps,** *Gray*, P. Z. S. 1866, p. 214. D. microps, Gray, *l. c.* 240, 395; Zool. E. & T. t. 25. *Hab.* Coast of Brazil.

3. **Clymenia Alope** (T. 32), *Gray*, P. Z. S. 1866, p. 214. D. Alope, Gray, *l. c.* 252, 399. *Hab.* Cape Horn.

4. **Clymenia Euphrosyne** (T. 22, 31), Gray, P. Z. S. 1866, p. 214. D. Euphrosyne, Gray, *l. c.* 251; Zool. E. & T. t. 22. *Hab.* North Sea.

4*. **Clymenia Styx** (Tab. 21). D. Styx, Gray, *l. c.* 250. *Hab.* West Africa.

*** *Beak of the skull once a half the length of the brain-case. Teeth large, four in an inch.* Gudamu.

5. **Clymenia gudamu.** Delphinus gudamu, *Owen, Trans. Zool. Soc.* vi. t. 3 (animal), t. 4 (skull). *Hab.* India (*W. Elliot*). Two skulls, B. M.
See Delphinus pomeegra, *Elliot, Journ. Asiat. Soc.* xvii. 250, xxviii. 491.

**** *Beak of the skull once and one-half or once and one-third the length of the brain-case. Teeth five or six in an inch.* Clymenia.

6. **Clymenia normalis.** Beak of the skull once and one-half the length of the brain-case, and as long as twice and one-half the width at the notch. Teeth 40, nearly six in an inch. Gray, P. Z. S. 1866, p. 214. Delphinus Clymene, Gray, *l. c.* 249.

7. **Clymenia Doris** (T. 20). Beak of the skull once and one-half the length of the brain-case, and as long as twice and a half the width at the notch. Teeth five in an inch. Gray, P. Z. S. 1866, p. 214. Tursio Doris, Gray, *l. c.* 255; Zool. E. & T. t. 20.

8. **Clymenia euphrosynoides.** Delphinus Euphrosyne, Gray (T. 31, skull); Owen, Trans. Zool. Soc. vi. t. 8. f. 5.

9. **Clymenia dorides.** Beak of the skull once and one-third the length of the brain-case, and as long as twice and one-third the width at the notch. Teeth five in an inch. Gray, P. Z. S. 1866, p. 215. Tursio dorides, Gray, *l. c.* 400. *Hab.* ——?

10. **Clymenia obscura** (T. 16, skull). Beak of the skull once and one-sixth the length of the brain-case, and as long as twice and one-half the width at the notch. Teeth five or six in an inch. The aperture of the blower large. Gray, P. Z. S. 1866, p. 215; 1868, fig. . Tursio obscurus, Gray, *l. c.* 264, 400; Zool. E. & T. t. 16. *Hab.* South Pacific.

11. **Clymenia similis,** Gray, P. Z. S. 1868, fig. . Skull like *C. obscura*, but palate contracted behind; side of pterygoid bone keeled. *Hab.* Cape of Good Hope.

III. SOTALIA, Gray, *l. c.* 393, 401.

Dorsal fin distinct. Beak depressed, rather longer than the brain-cavity. Teeth slender, conical. Palate flat behind. Pectoral fin ovate, obliquely truncated at the end; hand shorter than the arm-bones. Carpal bones small.

1. **Sotalia guianensis,** Gray, *l. c.* 401. Tursio guianensis, Gray, *l. c.* 257. *Hab.* British Guiana.

IV. DELPHINAPTERUS, Gray, *l. c.* 276.

Beak of skull elongate, depressed. Teeth small, slender. Dorsal fin none. Bladebone very broad, nearly semicircular.

1. **Delphinapterus Peronii** (T. 15, animal), Gray, *l. c.* 276. *Hab.* South Atlantic, New Guinea.

V. TURSIO, Gray, *l. c.* 254, 406; P. Z. S. 1866, p. 215.

Beak of the skull only rather longer than the brain-case, conical, convex above, rounded. Teeth large. Skull high. The skull large, thick, heavy, with a high swollen brain-cavity. The beak longer than the brain-case, broad, conical, stout, shelving on the sides. Teeth large, $\frac{22}{22}$ or $\frac{23}{23}$. The blower large. Nasal triangle produced considerably before the notch.

1. **Tursio truncatus,** Gray, *l. c.* 258, 406. no. 6; P. Z. S. 1866, p. 215. D. tursio, T. 10. f. 1. *Hab.* North Sea and Mediterranean.

2. **Tursio Metis** (T. 18), *Gray, l. c.* 256, no. 3; *Zool. E. & T.* t. 18; *P. Z. S.* 1866, p. 215. *Hab.* ——?

3. **Tursio Cymodoce** (T. 19), *Gray, l. c.* 257. no. 4; *Zool. E. & T.* t. 19; *P. Z. S.* 1866, p. 215. *Hab.* ——?

4. **Tursio Eurynome** (T. 17), *Gray, l. c.* 261. no. 8; *Zool. E. & T.* t. 17; *P. Z. S.* 1866, p. 215. *Hab.* South Sea, India?, Bay of Bengal.

5. **Tursio catalania**, *Gray, l. c.* 262. no. 10; *P. Z. S.* 1866, p. 215. *Hab.* North-west coast of Australia.
These skulls are all very much alike.

VI. EUTROPIA, *Gray, l. c.* 262; *P. Z. S.* 1866, p. 215.

Beak of the skull only rather longer than the brain-case. Skull depressed, thick, with the sides rather bent down behind the notch. The beak depressed, broad, rounded on the sides, rather longer than the length of the brain-case; the intermaxillaries flat, rather broad. Teeth small, slender, five or six in an inch.

The skull bears a considerable affinity to the skulls of *Phocæna*, *Neomeris*, *Beluga*, and *Monodon* in the bending down of the sides.

1. **Eutropia Dickiei** (T. 31), *Gray, P. Z. S.* 1866, p. 215. Tursio Eutropia, *Gray, P. Z. S.* 1862, p. 145; *l. c.* 262. no. 9. *Hab.* South Pacific Ocean, Chili.

2. **Eutropia Heavisidii**, *Gray, P. Z. S.* 1866, p. 215. Tursio Heavisidii, *Gray, l. c.* 263. *Hab.* From the Cape Seas.
The *D. cephalorhynchus* of F. Cuvier, judging from the figure of the skull given by Schlegel, appears also to belong to this genus.
See Stignatias (Amblyodon), *Cope, Proc. Acad. N. S. Philad.* 1866, p. 294.

VII. ORCAELLA, *Gray, l. c.* 285.

Animal ——? Dorsal fin ——? Pectoral fin ——? Skull :—brain-case subglobular; beak very short, two-thirds the length of brain-case, tapering, flat above. Intermaxillary half as wide as beak. Teeth small, conical, $\frac{5.5}{4.4}$.

1. **Orcaella brevirostris**, *Gray, l. c.* 285. Phocæna brevirostris, *Owen, Trans. Zool. Soc.* vi. t. 9. *Hab.* Indian Ocean.

Tribe III. LAGENORHYNCHINA.

Head attenuated, beaked. Beak of the skull as long as the length of the brain-case, broad, flat above; edges slightly reflexed and bent up in front of the notch. Nasal triangle elongate. Symphysis of the lower jaw short. *Lagenorhynchus*, Gray, *l. c.* 267.

I. ELECTRA, *Gray, l. c.* 267.

The beak of the skull very flat above, with the edges in front of the notches bent up. Teeth-line stopping considerably short of the notch.

* *Beak of the skull rather longer (about one-third) than the length of the brain-case. Teeth moderate, four in an inch, those in the lower jaw rather larger.*

1. **Electra obtusa**. Lagenorhynchus Electra (T. 13. skull), *Gray, l. c.* 268; *P. Z. S.* 1866, p. 216; *Zool. E. & T.* t. 13. Beak tapering, rounded in front. *Hab.*——?

2. **Electra Asia** (T. 14, skull). Lagenorhynchus Asia, *Gray, l. c.* 269. no. 3; *Zool. E. & T.* t. 14. Beak attenuated, acute in front. *Hab.* ——?

3. **Electra fusiformis**. Delphinus fusiformis, *Owen, Trans. Zool. Soc.* vi. t. 5. f. 1, t. 7 (skull). Beak broad, and rounded in front. *Hab.* India (*W. Elliot*). B.M.

4. **Electra acuta**. Lagenorhynchus acutus, *Gray, l. c.* 269. no. 4, according to Schlegel's figure of the skull, should be arranged in this section. *Hab.* North Sea.

** *Beak of the skull rather shorter than the length of the brain-cavity. Teeth small, five or six in an inch.*

5. **Electra clancula** (T. 35). Lagenorhynchus clanculus, *Gray, l. c.* 271, 272, 275. Beak of the skull broad behind, once and three-fourths the width of the notch in length. Teeth five in an inch. *Hab.* South Pacific Ocean.

6. **Electra thicolea** (T. 36). Lagenorhynchus thicolea, *Gray, l. c.* 271. no. 7. Beak of the skull narrow behind, twice as long as the width at the notch. Teeth small, six in an inch. *Hab.* West coast of North America.

II. LEUCOPLEURUS, *Gray, P. Z. S.* 1866, p. 216.

Beak of the skull rather flat above and elongate, bent up on the edge in front of the notch, narrow behind, as long as, or slightly longer than, the length of the brain-case. Teeth-line reaching nearly to the notch. Teeth small, five in an inch. First and second cervical vertebræ united by their bodies, third and fourth by the spinous processes.

1. **Leucopleurus arcticus** (T. 6. f. 3, 5, fœtus; T. 12 skull; T. 26. f. 3, tongue). Lagenorhynchus leucopleurus, *Gray, l. c.* 273. no. 9. Beak of the skull twice as long as the width at the notch. Teeth small, five in an inch. *Hab.* North Sea.

III. LAGENORHYNCHUS, *Gray, P. Z. S.* 1866, p. 216; *l. c.* 272.

Beak of the skull rather flat above, bent up on the edges

in front of the notch, deep, broad behind, rather shorter than the length of the brain-case. Teeth-line reaching nearly to the notch, large, three in an inch. First and second cervical vertebræ united by their bodies; the third, fourth, fifth, six, and seventh free.

1. **Lagenorhynchus albirostris** (T. 10. f. 2, T. 11, skull), *Gray, l. c.* 272. no. 8. The beak of the skull once and one-half as long as the width at the notch. *Hab.* North Sea, Yarmouth.

Tribe IV. PHOCÆNINA.

Head rounded in front, scarcely beaked. Beak of skull depressed, broad, scarcely so long as the brain-cavity.

* *Lateral wing of the maxilla horizontally produced over the orbits. Dorsal distinct. Teeth conical.*

I. PSEUDORCA.

Triangle in front of the blowers flat. Teeth large, conical, acute, permanent.

1. **Pseudorca crassidens**, *Gray, l. c.* 290. no. 1. *Hab.* North Sea.

2. **Pseudorca meridionalis**, *Gray, l. c.* 291. no. 2, figs. 58, 59. *Hab.* Van Diemen's Land.

** *Lateral wing of the maxilla shelving down over the orbit. Triangle in front of the blower convex. Teeth compressed.*

II. PHOCÆNA, *Gray, l. c.* 301.

Dorsal fin distinct, in the middle of the back, with a series of small spines on the upper part of its front edge. Teeth all compressed, truncate.

1. **Phocæna communis**, *Gray, l. c.* 302. Var.? Phocæna tuberculifera, *Gray, l. c.* 304. *Hab.* North Sea.

III. ACANTHODELPHIS, *Gray, l. c.* 304.

Dorsal fin distinct, rather behind the middle of the back. Back in front of the dorsal fin with a single, and the upper part of the front edge of the dorsal fin with three, series of oblong keeled tubercles. Teeth compressed, front one rather conical.

1. **Acanthodelphis spinipennis**, *Gray, l. c.* 304. *Hab.* Coast of Brazil.

VII. NEOMERIS, *Gray, l. c.* 306.

Dorsal fin none.

1. **Neomeris phocænoides**, *Gray, l. c.* 306. Hab Indian Ocean, Bengal, Cape of Good Hope, Japan. "Delphinus molagan," *Owen, Trans. Zool. Soc.* vi. 24, a name given to a manuscript note of Mr. Elliot's!

2. *Pectoral fin large, broad, rounded at the end; ham shorter than the arm-bones; carpal bones single, immerse in a large cartilage. Phalanges of the index-finger eigh*

Tribe V. ORCADINA.

1. ORCA, *Gray, l. c.* 278.

Head rounded, scarcely beaked. Dorsal fin falcat Skull heavy; rings of side expanded; beak short, broad triangle in front of the blowers flat; teeth large.

* *Beak broad, oblong; intermaxillaries half as broad as beak. Lower jaw narrow in front. Orca.*

1. **Orca gladiator**, *Gray, l. c.* 279. *Hab.* North Se

2. **Orca intermedia** (T. 8, skull), *Gray, l. c.* 28 *Hab.* ——?

3. **Orca magellanica**, *Burmeister, Ann. & Mag. N. H* xviii. 101, t. 9. f. 5. *Hab.* Buenos Ayres.
See *O. destructor*, Cope, Proc. Acad. N. S. Philad. 186 p. 293. Peru.

** *Beak oblong, trigonal; intermaxillaries narrow, not ha as wide as beak. Lower jaw thick in front.* Ophysia.

4. **Orca capensis** (T. 9, skull), *Gray, l. c.* 283. Ha Southern Ocean, Cape of Good Hope.

Family X. GLOBIOCEPHALIDÆ, *Gray, l. c.* 62, 312

Head blunt, very much swollen. Teeth in the front part both jaws, cylindrical, simple. Dorsal fin falcat Pectoral fin low down on the sides of the body; fi gers elongate, many-jointed.

I. GLOBIOCEPHALUS, *Gray, l. c.* 313.

Skull—palate flat; beak rather tapering in front; fir to sixth cervical vertebræ anchylosed into one mass.

* *Black, with a white streak beneath.*

1. **Globiocephalus svineval**, *Gray, l. c.* 314. Pil Whale. *Hab.* North Sea, coast of England.
See 1. Globiocephalus Edwardsii, *Gray, l. c.* 320. Ha Cape of Good Hope; coloured exactly like that of North Se

2. Globiocephalus Grayii, *Burmeister, Ann. & Mag. N. H.* 1868, p. 52, t. 2. f. 2, 3. *Hab.* Buenos Ayres.

** *Black, or only slightly paler beneath.*

2. **Globiocephalus macrorhynchus**, *Gray, l. c.* 320. *Hab.* South Seas.

See 1. Globiocephalus indicus, *Gray, l. c.* 322. *Hab.* Bay of Bengal. 2. Globiocephalus Sieboldii, *Gray, l. c.* 323. *Hab.* Japan.

II. Sphærocephalus, *Gray, l. c.* 323.

Palate of the skull convex, shelving on the sides. Beak oblong, of nearly the same width the greater part of its height.

1. **Sphærocephalus incrassatus**, *Gray, l. c.* 324 (figures). *Hab.* British Channel, Bridport.

Family XI. BELUGIDÆ.

Head rounded in front (or very shortly beaked). Teeth in both jaws more or less early deciduous, rarely wanting, or, rather, not developed. Back sometimes with a compressed dorsal fin, often wanting. Skull with the lateral expansion of the maxilla over the orbit, and the side of the beak shelving downwards.

* *Dorsal fin distinct. Pectoral fin subelongate.*

I. Grampus, *Gray, l. c.* 230, 295, 393.

Skull lateral; wings of the maxilla over the orbit horizontal. Intermaxilla broad; triangle in front of the blowers convex. Teeth conical; upper early deciduous. Pectoral fin ovate, falcate. Cervical vertebræ anchylosed.

† *Triangle in front of the blowers elongate, produced in front over the vomer.*

1. **Grampus Cuvieri**, *Gray, l. c.* 295 (figure). *Hab.* North Sea, Hampshire.

†† *Triangle in front of the blower short, broad.*

2. **Grampus Richardsonii**, *Gray, l. c.* 299. *Hab.* Cape of Good Hope.

** *Dorsal fin none. Pectoral fin ovate, small.*

II. Beluga, *Gray, l. c.* 232, 306, 393.

Lateral wing of the maxilla over the orbit shelving downward. Teeth conical in both jaws, early deciduous. Male without any spiral hornlike tooth.

1. **Beluga catodon** (Tab. 29. f. 3, tongue), *Gray, l. c.* 307, fig 64. Delphinus canadensis, T. 5, head false, with beak. *Hab.* North Sea, mouths of rivers.

2. **Beluga Kingii** (T. 7), *Gray, l. c.* 309. *Hab.* Australia.

III. Monodon, *Gray, l. c.* 234, 310, 393.

Lateral expansion over the orbit shelving down. Teeth in both jaws very early deciduous. Male with one, rarely two, very long, projecting, spiral tusks in the left side of the upper jaw. Cervical vertebræ—first free, thin; second and third united by the spinal processes.

1. **Monodon monoceros**, *Gray, l. c.* 311. *Hab.* North Sea.

Suborder VI. ZIPHIOIDEA.

(*Ziphiidæ*, Gray, l. c. 62, 326.)

Head beaked. Nostrils two, united into a single transverse or crescent-like blower on the centre of the back of the crown. Teeth only in the front or side of the lower jaw, fitting into pits in the upper one. Dorsal fin falcate. Pectoral fin ovate, small, low down on the side of the body; fingers four- or five-jointed. Cervical vertebræ united into one mass.

Family XII. HYPEROODONTIDÆ.

(*Hyperoodontina*, Gray, l. c. 327.)

Blower lunate. Beak of the skull with a high crest on each side above, formed by the elevation of the maxillary bones in front of the blower. Teeth two or four, in front of the lower jaw, conical. Cervical vertebræ united into one mass.

I. Hyperoodon, *Gray, l. c.* 327, 328.

Beak of the skull bent downwards; crest of the back of the beak sharp-edged, above as high as the occiput.

1. **Hyperoodon butzkopf** (T. 3), *Gray, l. c.* 330. H. rostratum, T. 3. *Hab.* North Sea.

II. Lagenocetus, *Gray, l. c.* 327, 336.

Beak of the skull straight, erect at the beak, very large, flattened, higher than the occiput.

1. **Lagenocetus latifrons**, *Gray, l. c.* 339. Hyperoodon latifrons, T. 1. *Hab.* North Sea.

Family XIII. EPIODONTIDÆ.

(*Epiodontina*, Gray, l. c. 327.)

Blower lunate. Skull—beak ——?; maxillaries simple,

not dilated above; intermaxillaries enlarged behind, forming a more or less deep cavity round the nostrils. Teeth two or four in front of the lower jaw, conical or cylindrical. Cervical vertebræ—first, second, and third united into one mass, which is produced and truncated above; rest thin, free.

I. EPIODON, *Gray, l. c.* 327, 340.

Skull—vomer simple, small; intermaxillaries elevated, and forming a moderately deep, well-marked basin round the nostrils. Fingers 5; carpal bones 6, phalanges 2, 3, 4, 3, 3. Sternal bones separate from front, lanceolate. Vertebræ 42, the 11 front caudal with chevron bone.

1. **Epiodon Desmarestii,** *Gray, l.c.* 341. *Hab.* North Sea and Mediterranean.

2. **Epiodon cryptodon,** *Burmeister, Ann. & Mag. N. H.* xvii. 94, t. 5, 6; *Anat. Mus. Buenos Ayres,* t. 15-21. *Hab.* Buenos Ayres.

II. PETRORHYNCHUS, *Gray, l. c.* 327, 342.

Skull trigonal. Vomer swollen, forming a large, elongated tubercle between the callous intermaxillaries. Intermaxillaries forming a deep basin round the nostrils.

1. **Petrorhynchus capensis,** *Gray, l. c.* 346 (figs. 67, 68). Ziphius indicus, *Van Beneden* (fig. 69). *Hab.* South Seas, Cape Seas.

Family XIV. ZIPHIIDÆ.
(*Ziphiina,* Gray, *l. c.* 327, 348.)

Skull beaked. Maxillaries not dilated above. Intermaxillaries linear, rather swollen on the sides of the nostrils. Teeth on the side of the lower jaw compressed.

I. BERARDIUS, *Gray, l. c.* 327, 348.

Teeth 4, in the front of the side of the lower jaw, conical, compressed. Lower jaw gradually tapering in front.

1. **Berardius arnuxi,** *Gray, l. c.* 348 (fig. 70). *Hab.* New Zealand.

II. ZIPHIUS, *Gray, l. c.* 327.

Teeth 2, in the middle of the side of the lower jaw. Teeth of the male short, truncated at the end; of female small, curved. Lower jaw gradually tapering in front.

1. **Ziphius Sowerbiensis,** *Gray, l. c.* 350, fig. 71 (Tab. 5. f. 3, 4, skull). *Hab.* British Channel, Irish Sea.

III. DOLICHODON, *Gray, l. c.* 353.

Teeth 2, in the middle of the side of the lower jaw. Teeth (of male) very long, strap-shaped, produced, arched obliquely, truncated at the end, with a conical process on the front of the terminal edge.

1. **Dolichodon Layardii.** Ziphius Layardii, *Gray, l. c.* 353 (fig. 72). *Hab.* Cape of Good Hope.

IV. DIOPLODON, *Gray, l. c.* 327, 355.

Teeth 2 or 4, conical, in the middle of the side of the lower jaw. Lower jaw broad behind, suddenly contracted in front.

1. **Dioplodon sechellensis** (T. 5. f. 4), *Gray, l. c.* 357. Ziphius Sechellensis, T. 6. f. 1, 2, skull. *Hab.* Seychelles. Mus. Paris.

This Synopsis is strictly confined to the species of Whales and Dolphins which I have been able to examine, compare, and characterize. Sometimes only small portions of the skeletons of the animals have come under my examination; but the parts so examined have been carefully compared with similar parts of the known species and their distinctness proved before they were inserted in the Synopsis. Unfortunately it is very difficult to obtain even portions of the skeleton of the Cetacea, and one must follow the method of the palæontologist and establish genera and species on such specimens as one can obtain, waiting for more perfect material to be obtained; the result of such work has been very satisfactory.

The number of Cetacea will be very much extended; for after establishing the species from the examination and comparison of the bones, there will have to be described the species that have similar bones, and yet have very different external characters; and, if we may judge from the species of the restricted genus *Delphinus* which have been examined and compared, species so distinguished will be numerous. More than half of the Plates have appeared in the 'Voyage of the Erebus and Terror.'

The student is referred for more details to the catalogue of 'Seals and Whales in the British Museum,' 8vo, 1866. Consult also Professor Lilljeborg on two subfossil Whales discovered in Sweden, Upsala, 1867, from Nova Acta Roy. Acad. Scien. of Upsala, vol. vi. 1867, and my paper on the "Geographical Distribution of the Right Whales," Ann. & Mag. Nat. Hist. 1868, ser. 4. i. p. 242.

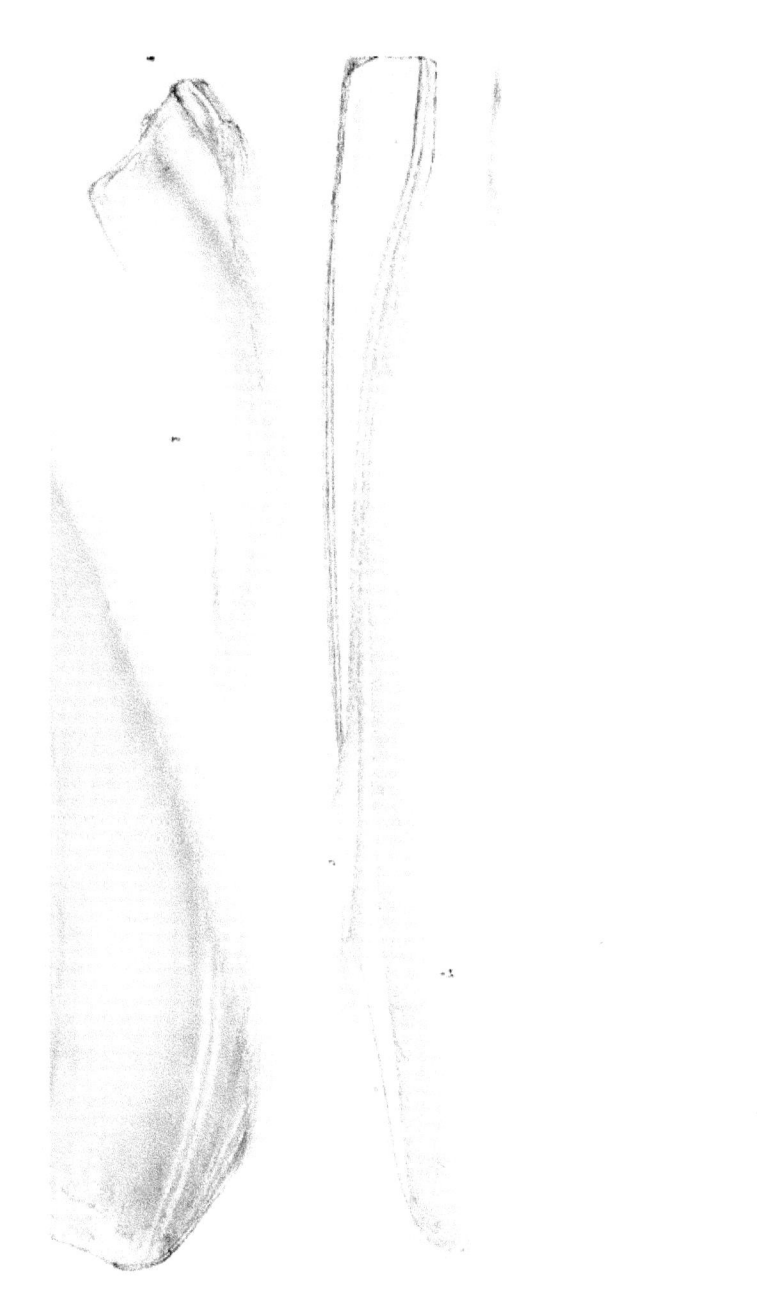

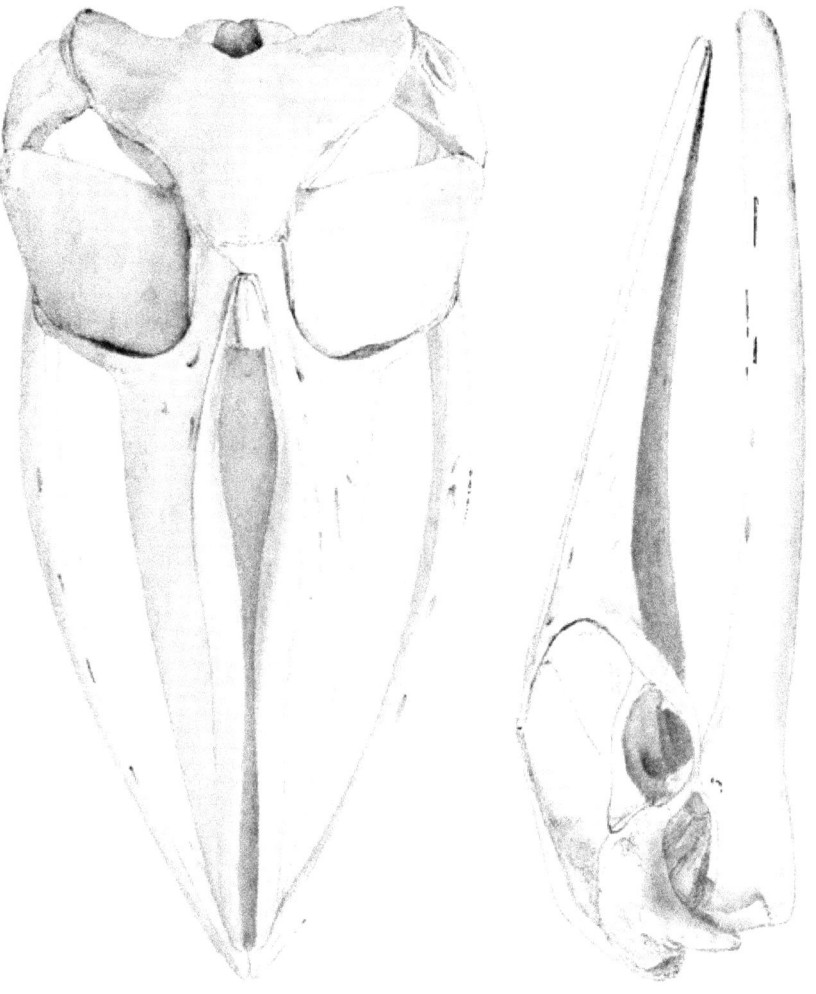

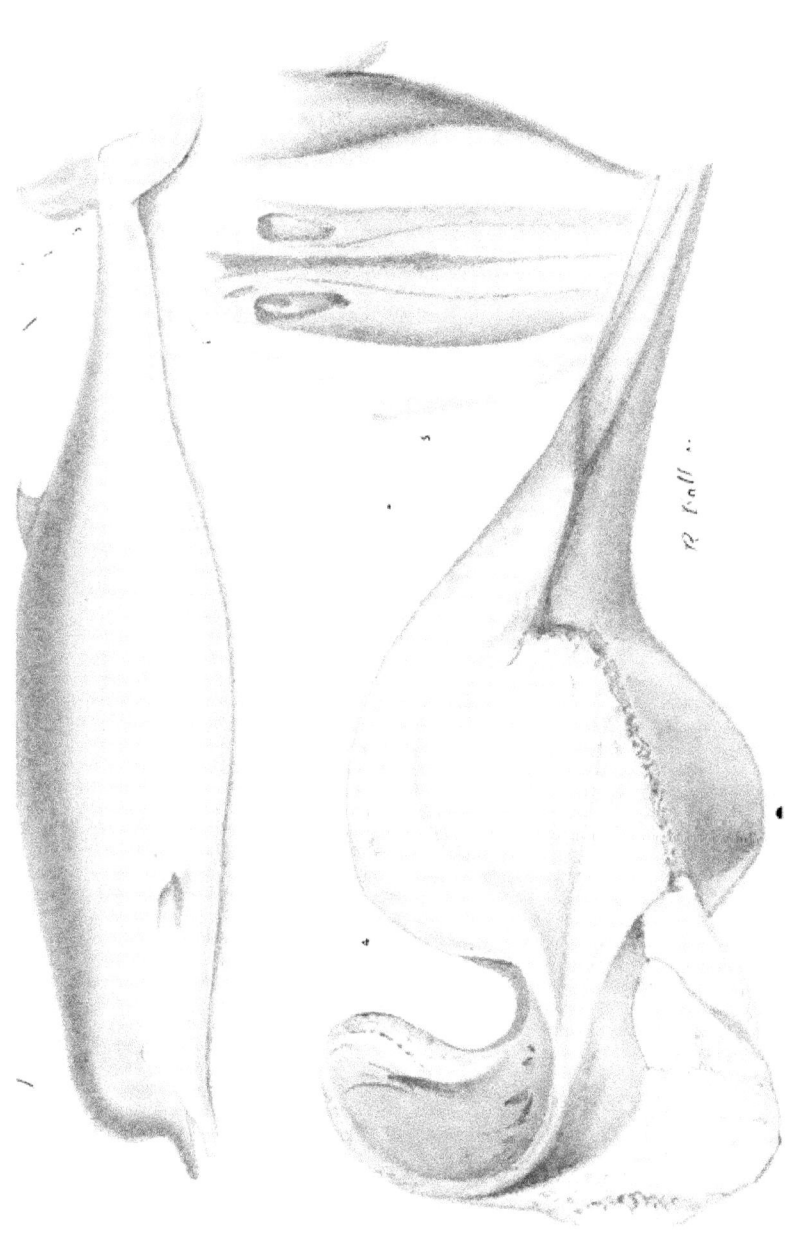

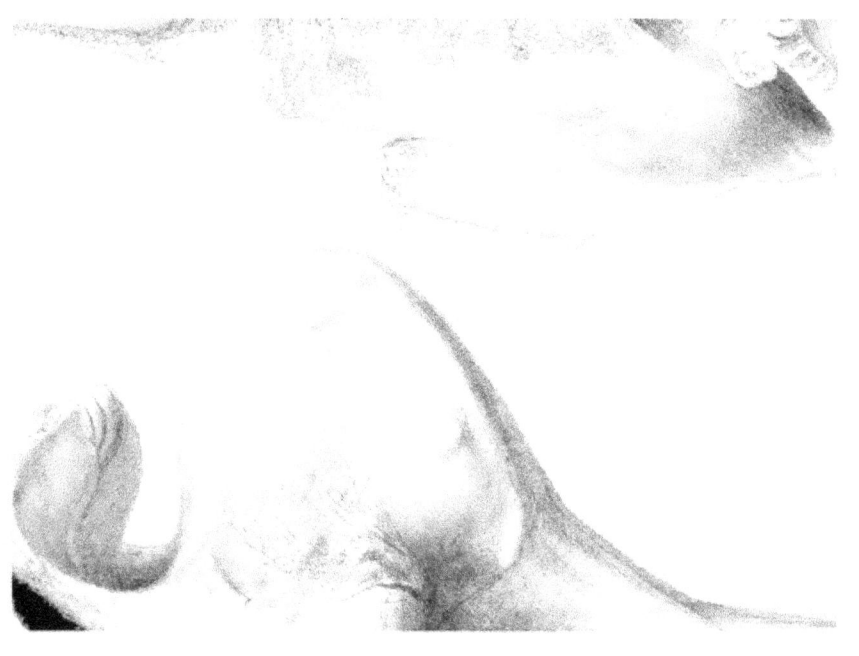

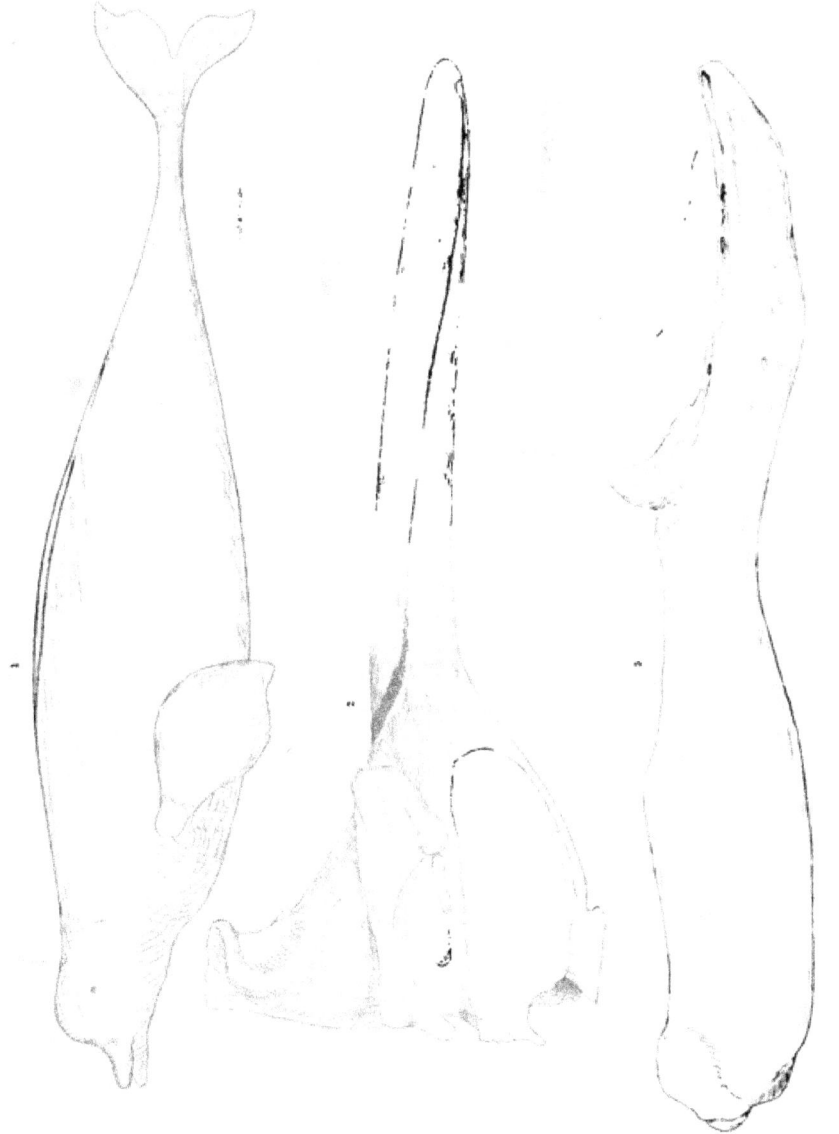

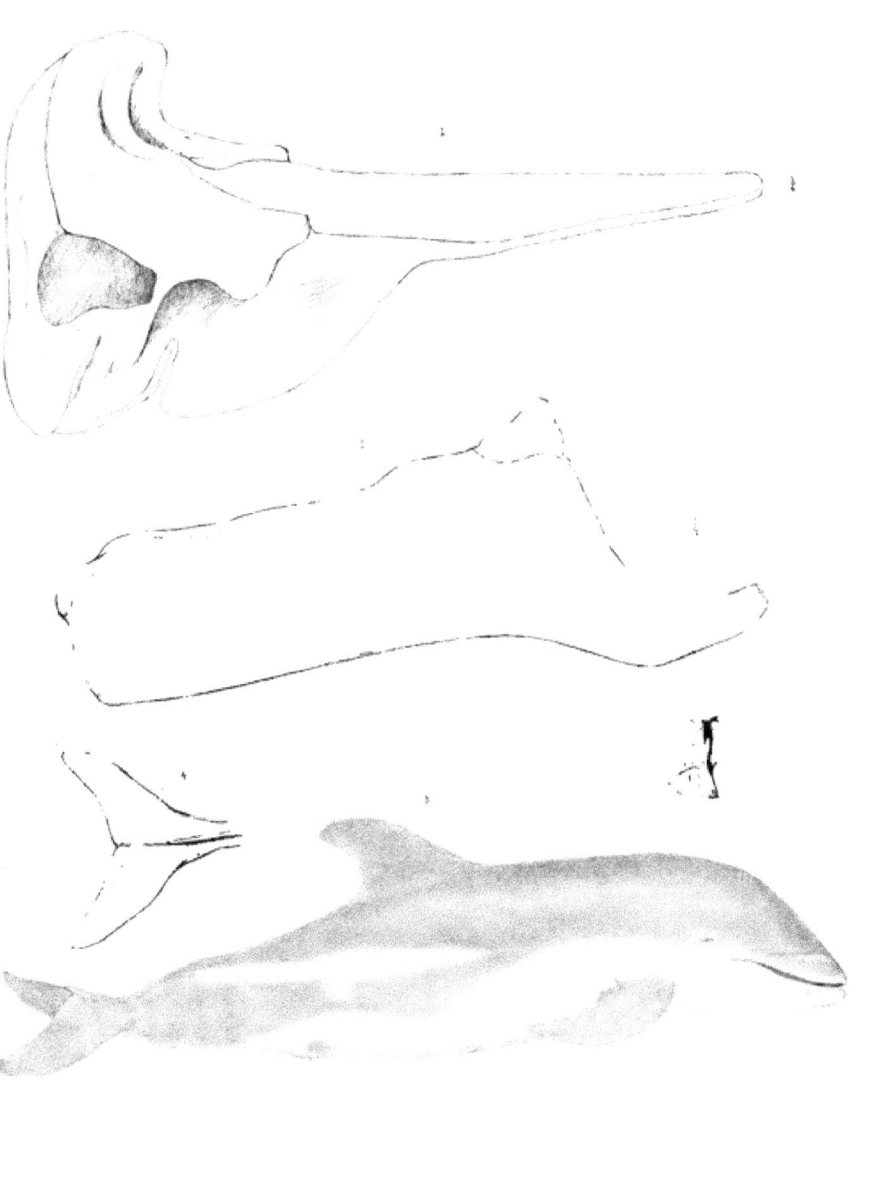

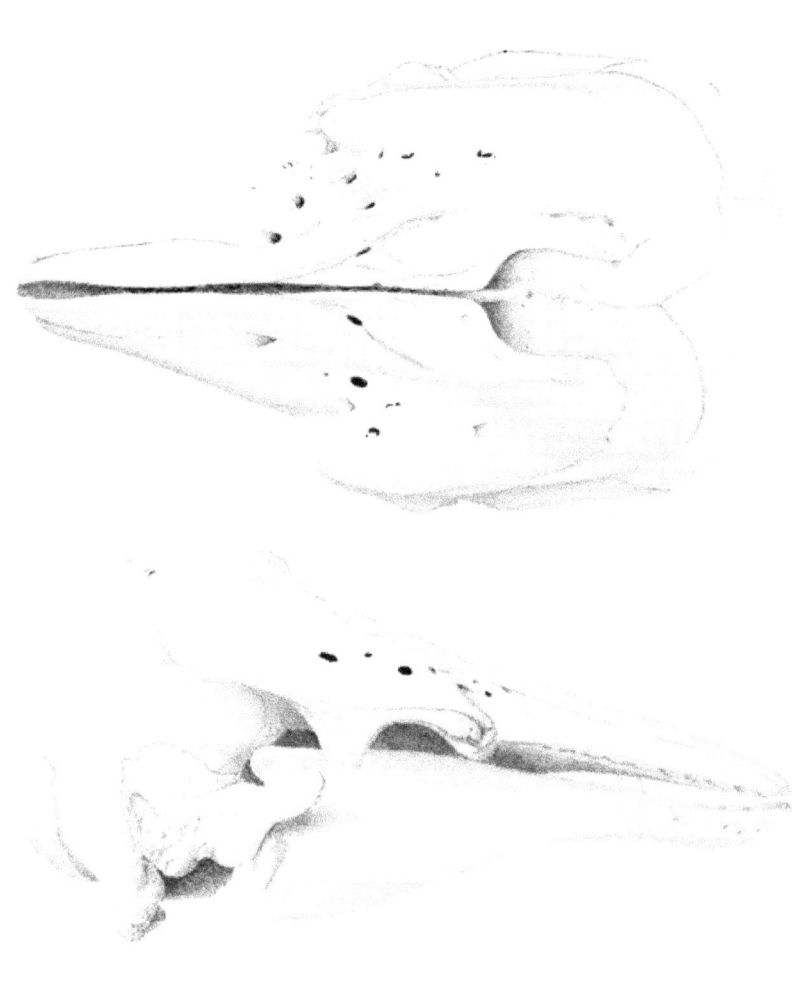

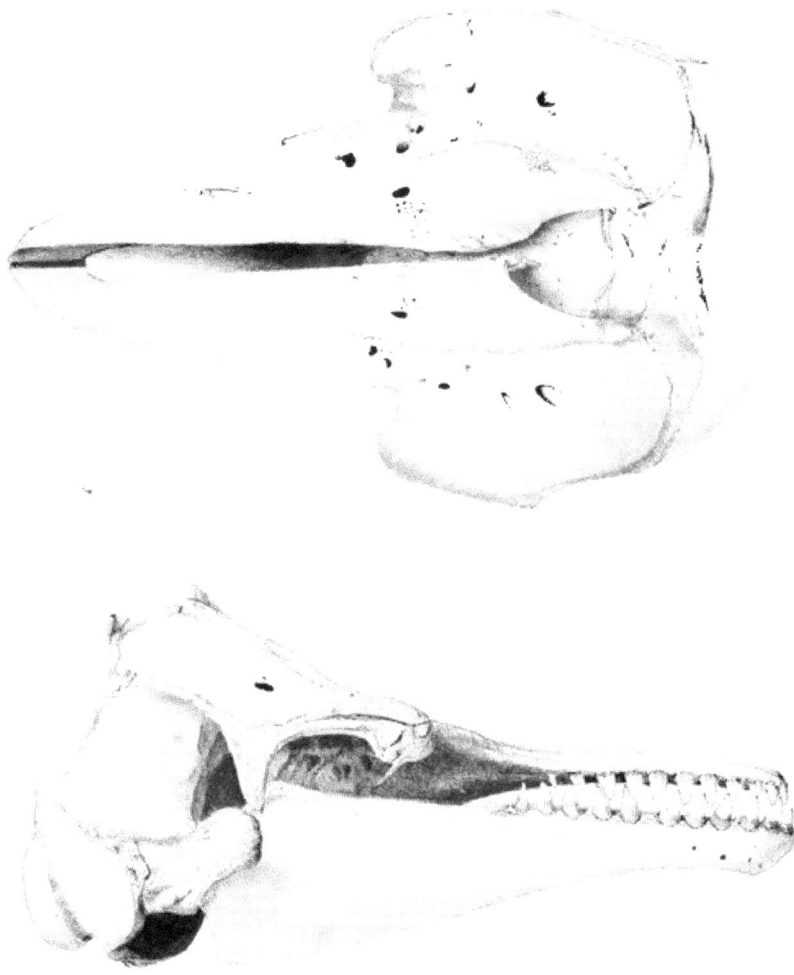

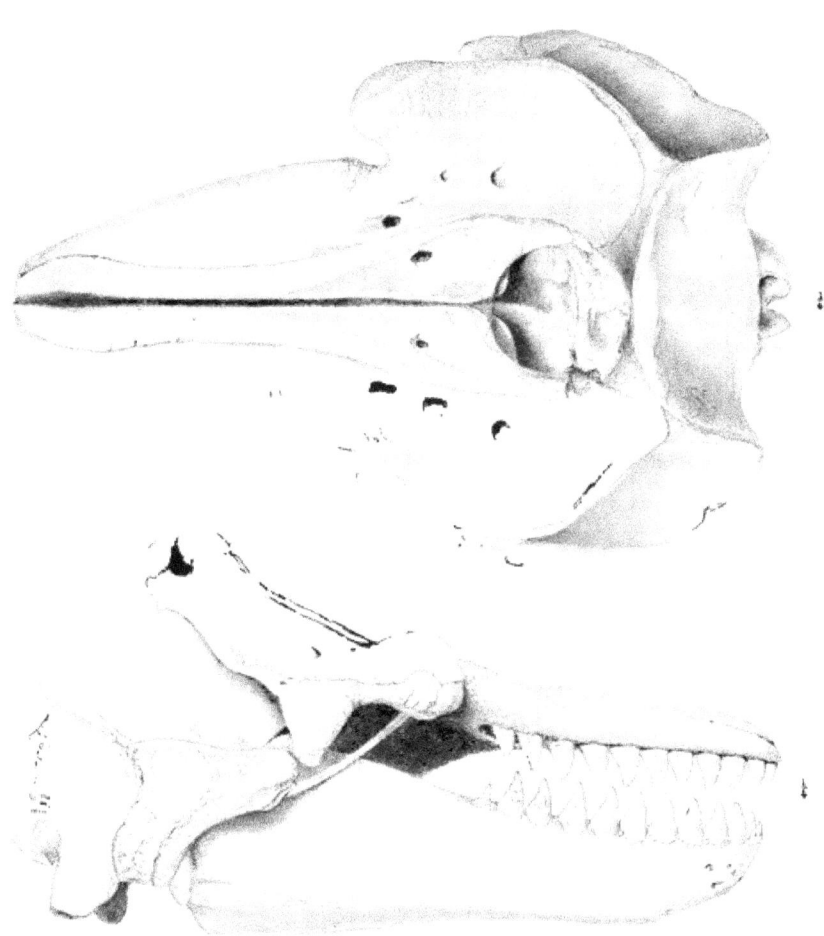

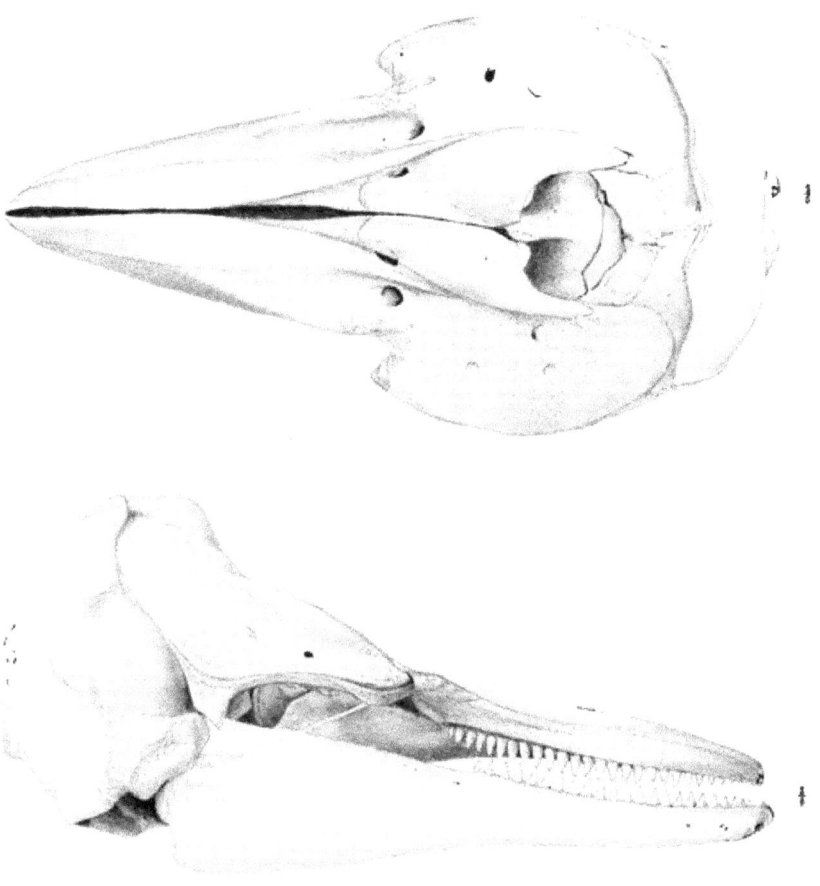

WHITE LIPPED BOTTLE-NOSE LAGENORHYNCHUS ALBIROSTRIS

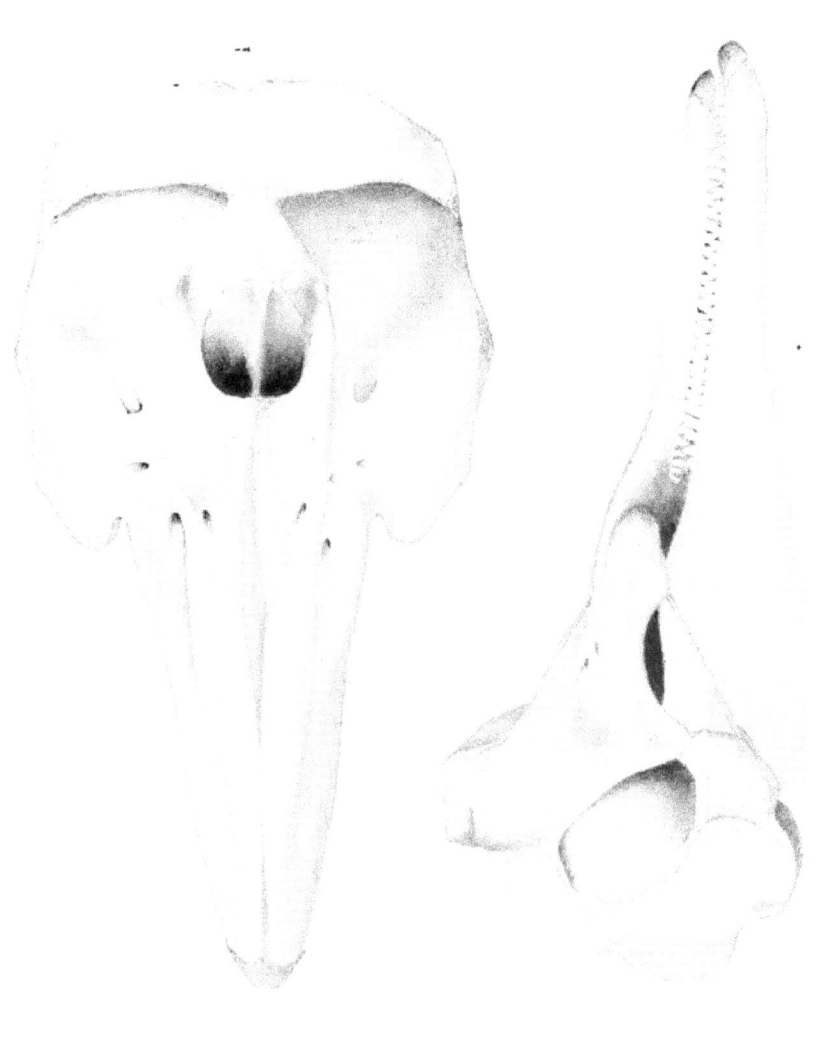

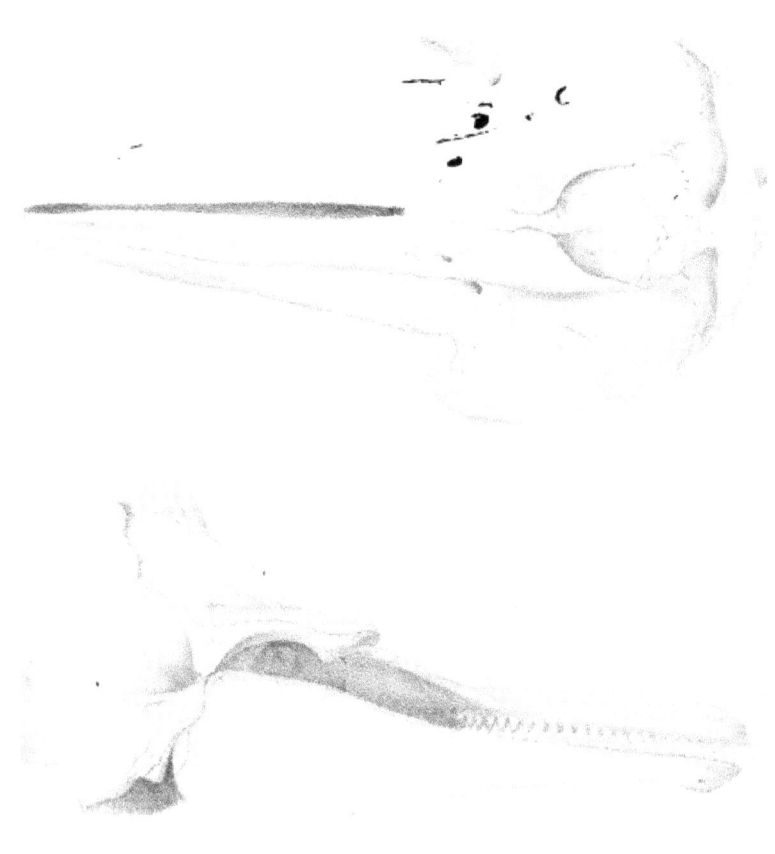

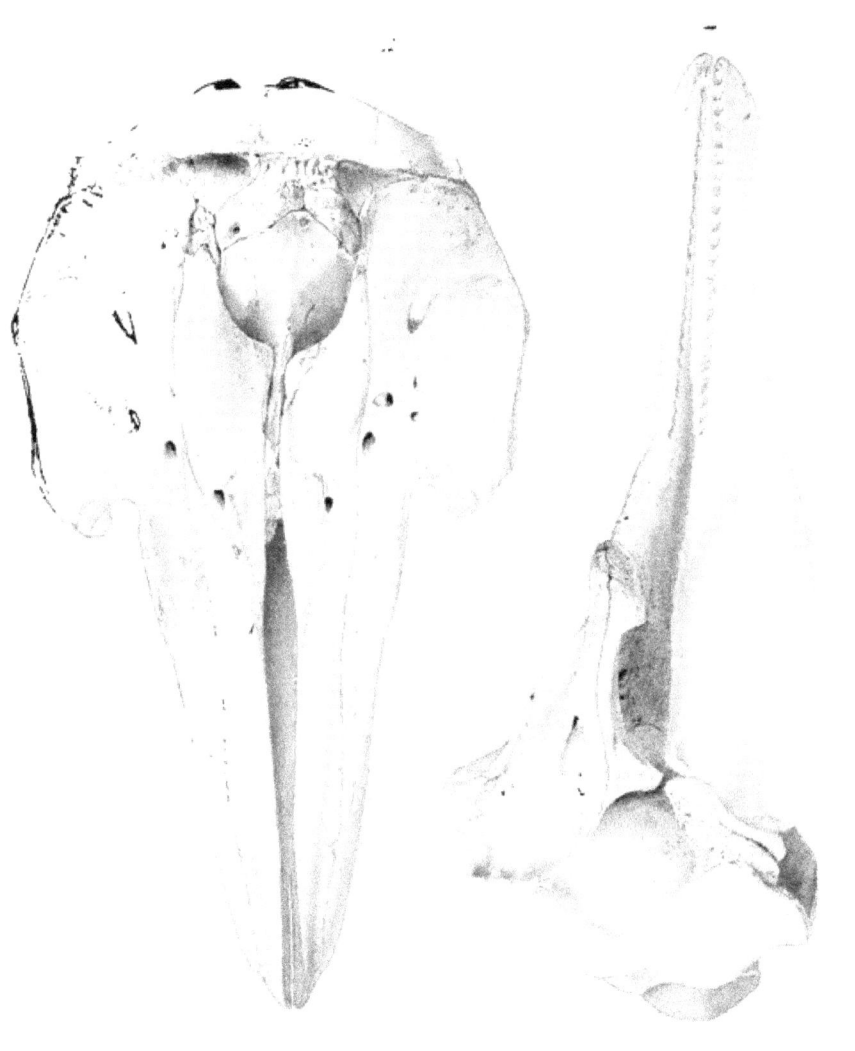

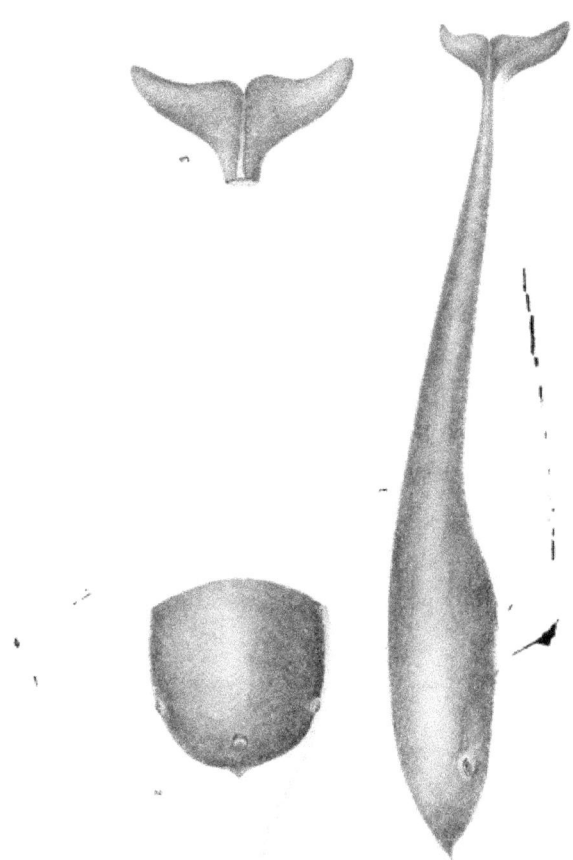

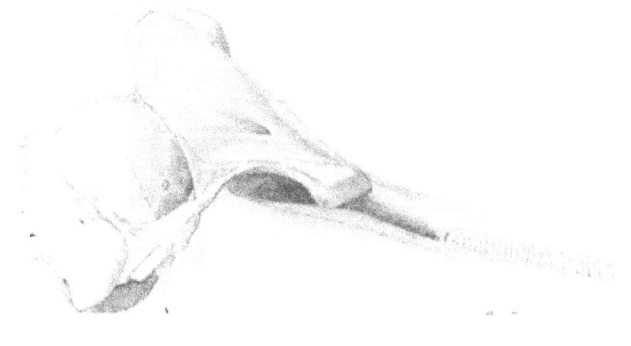

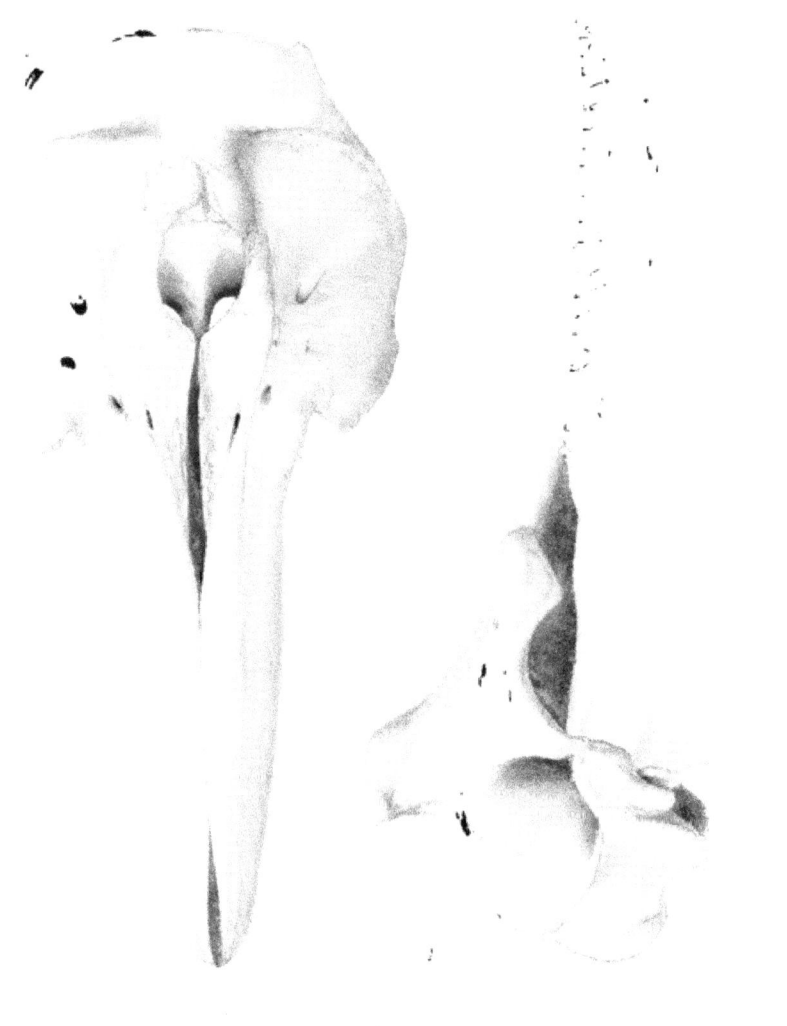

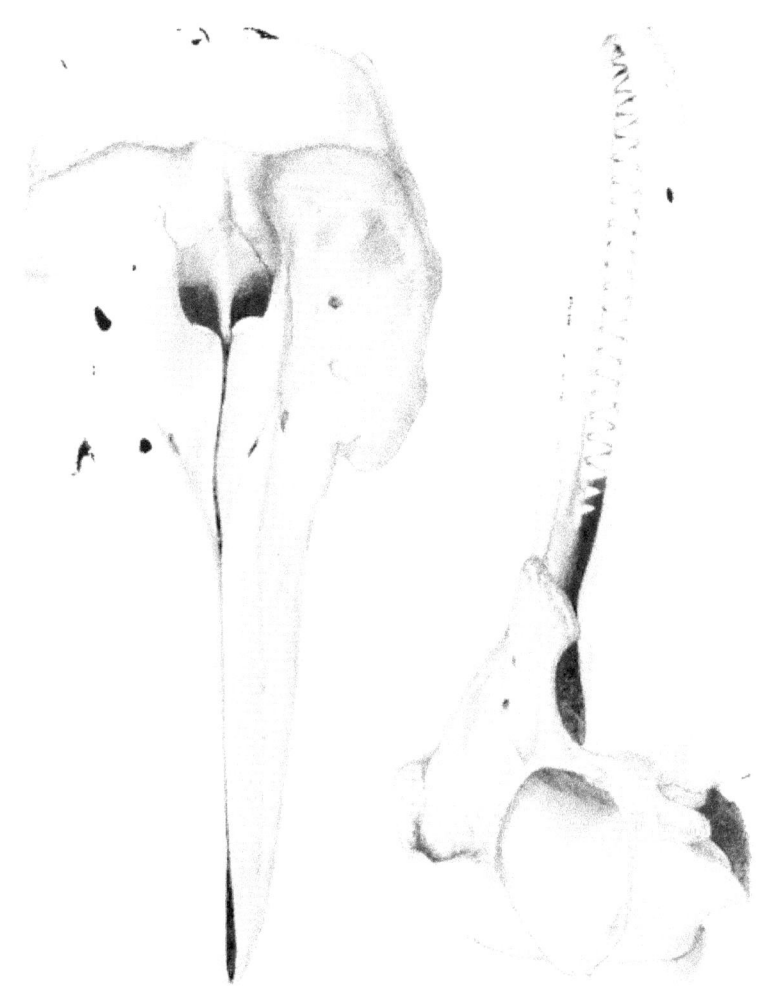

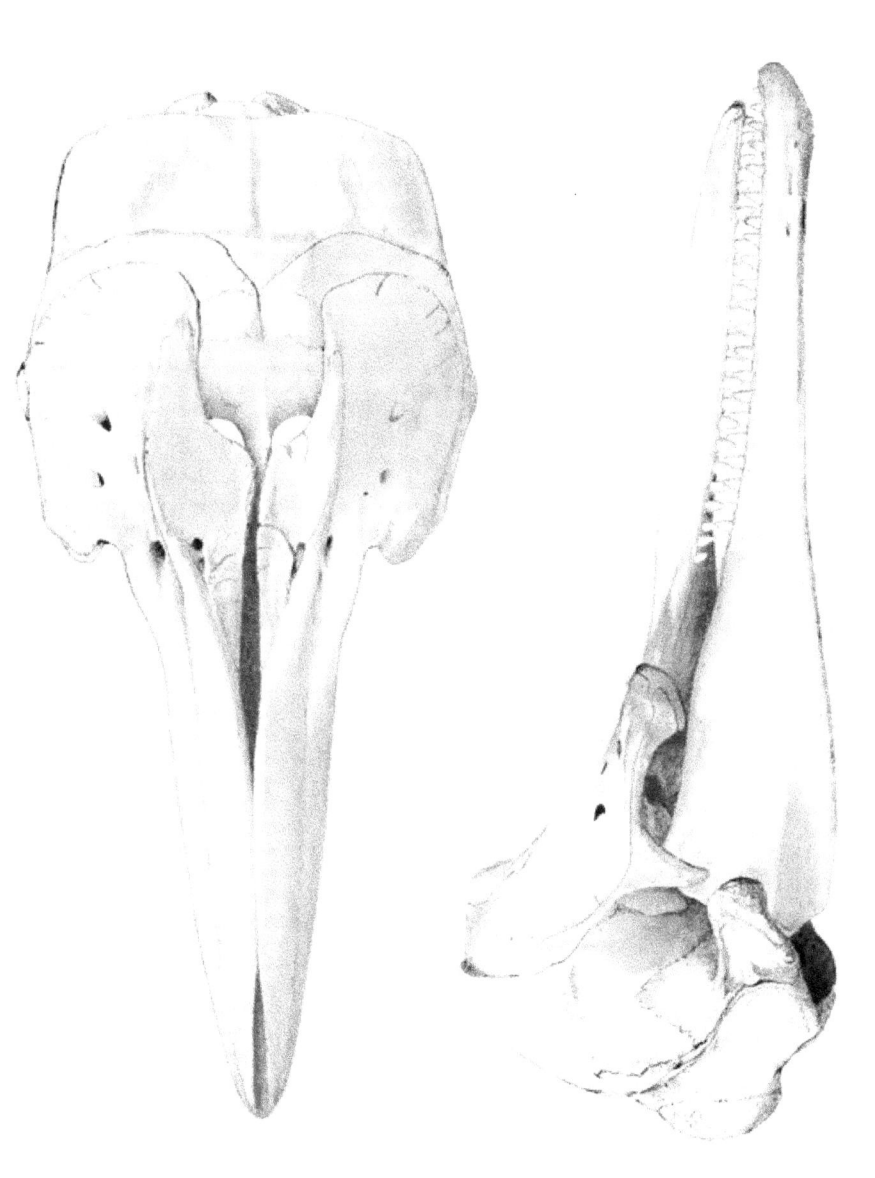

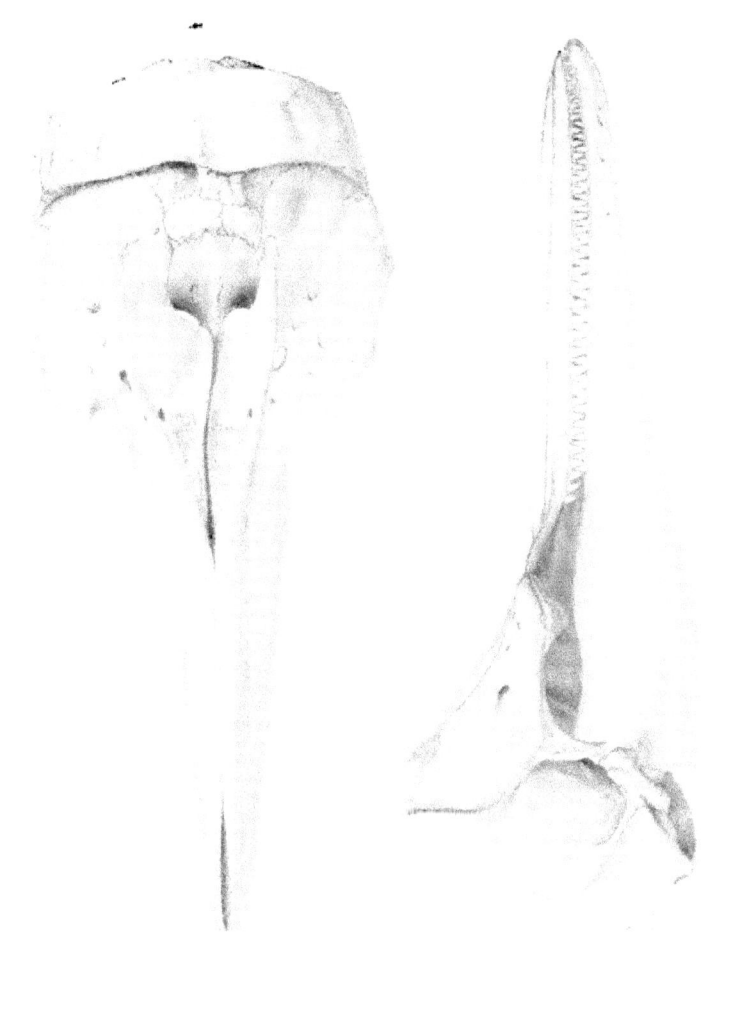

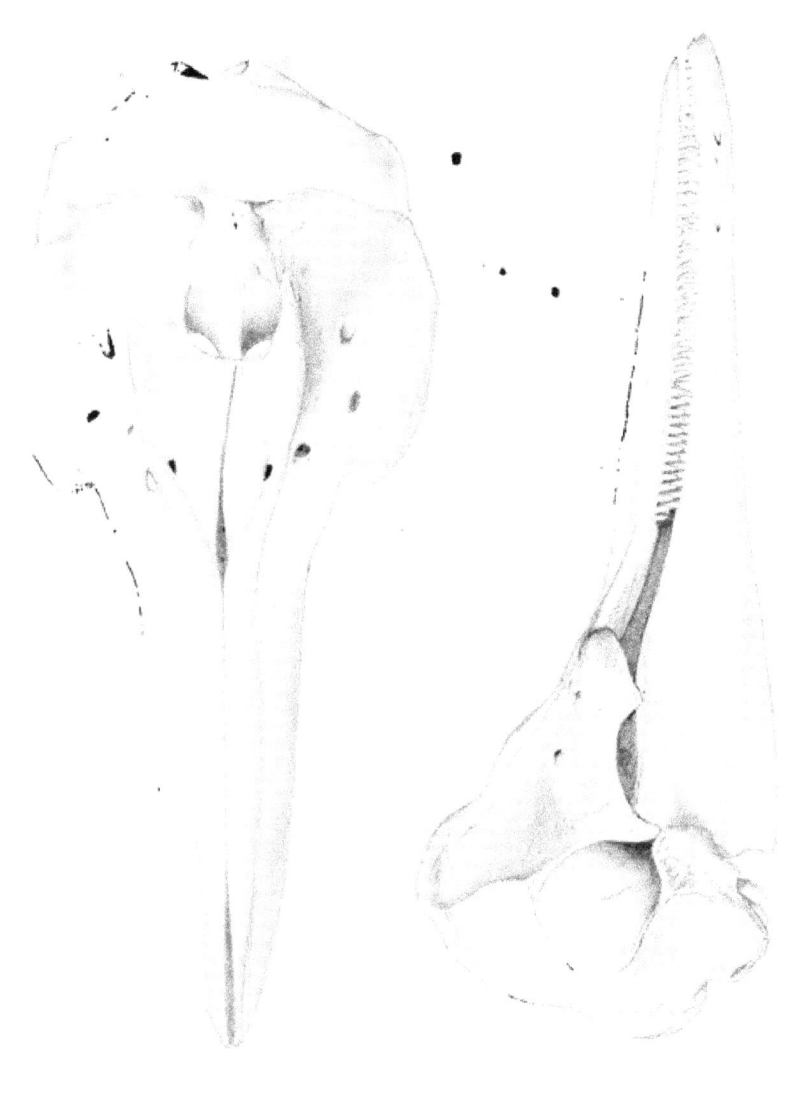

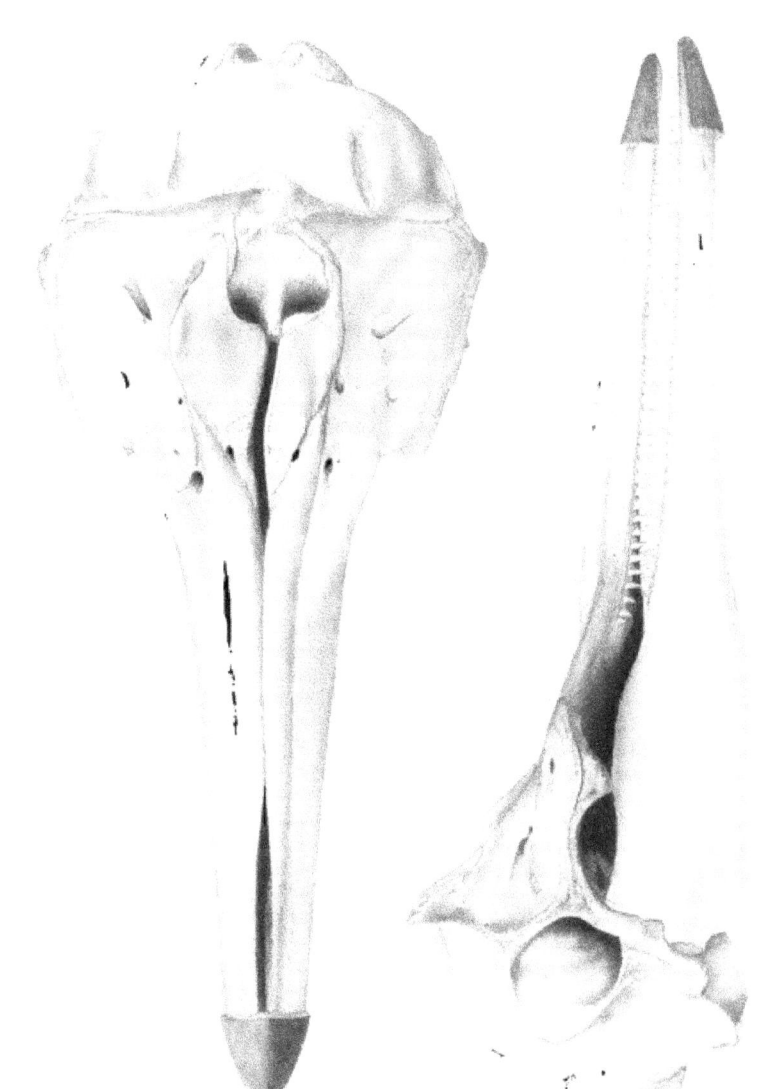

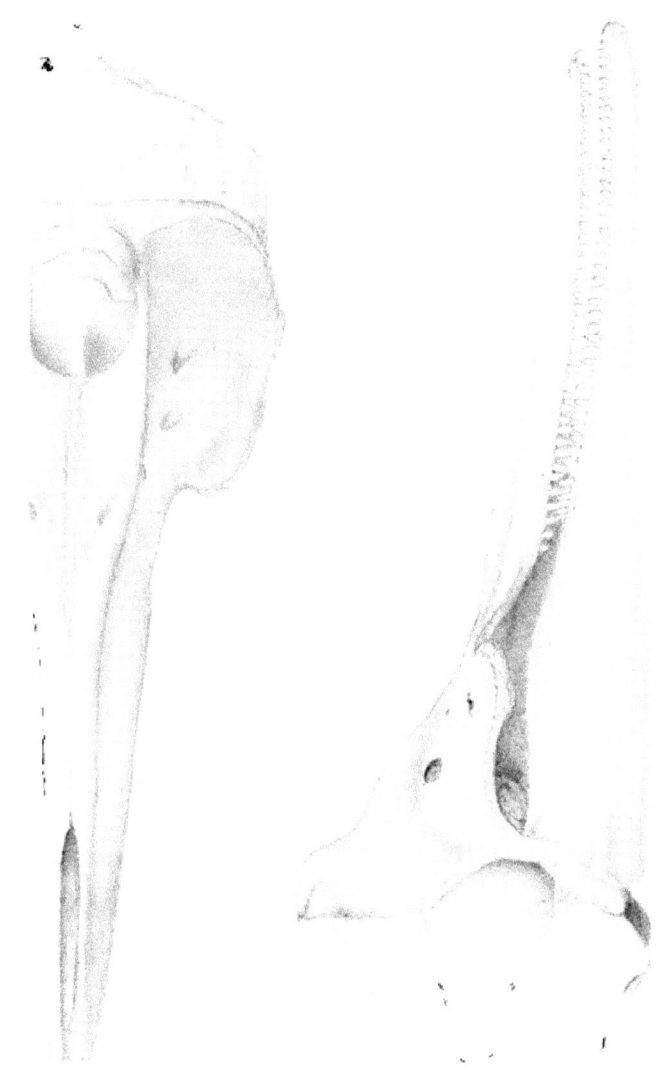

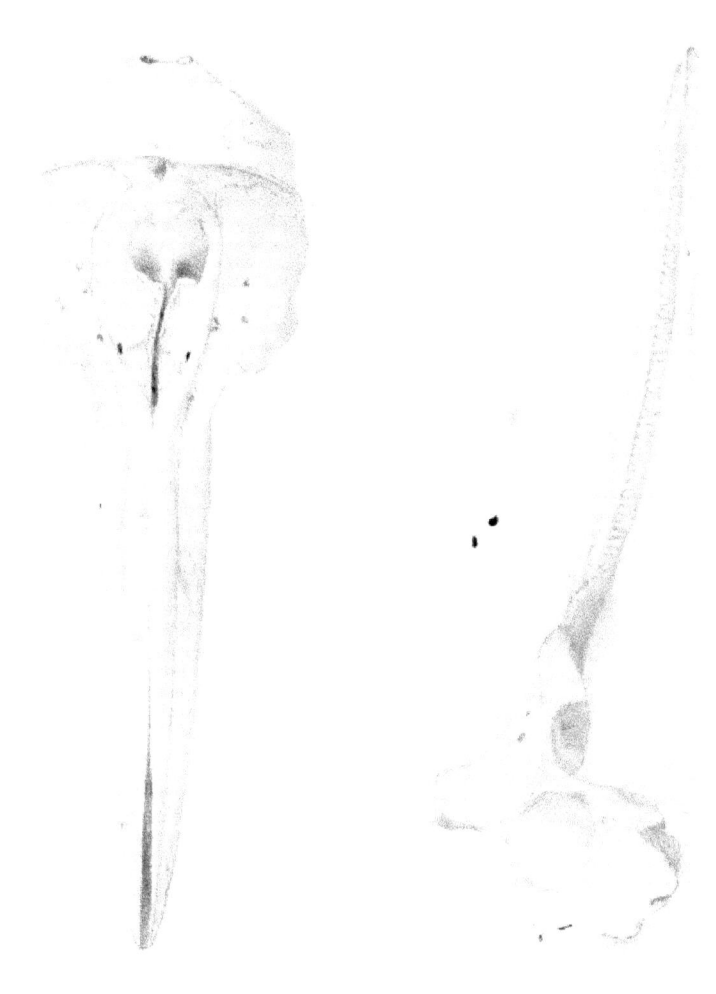

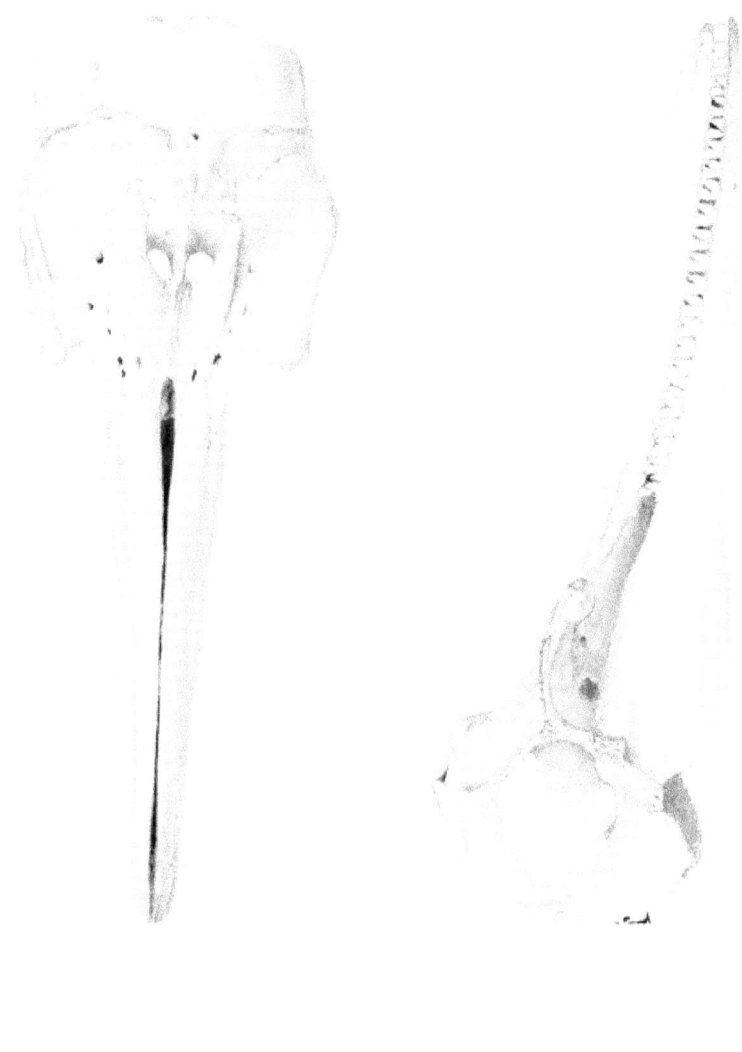

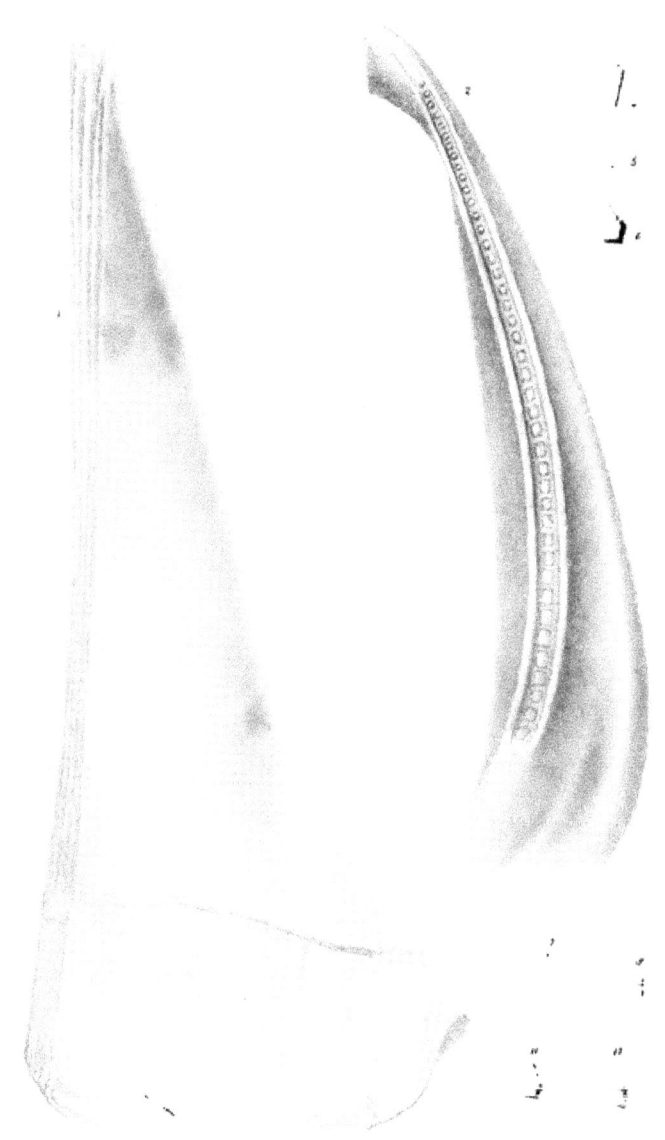

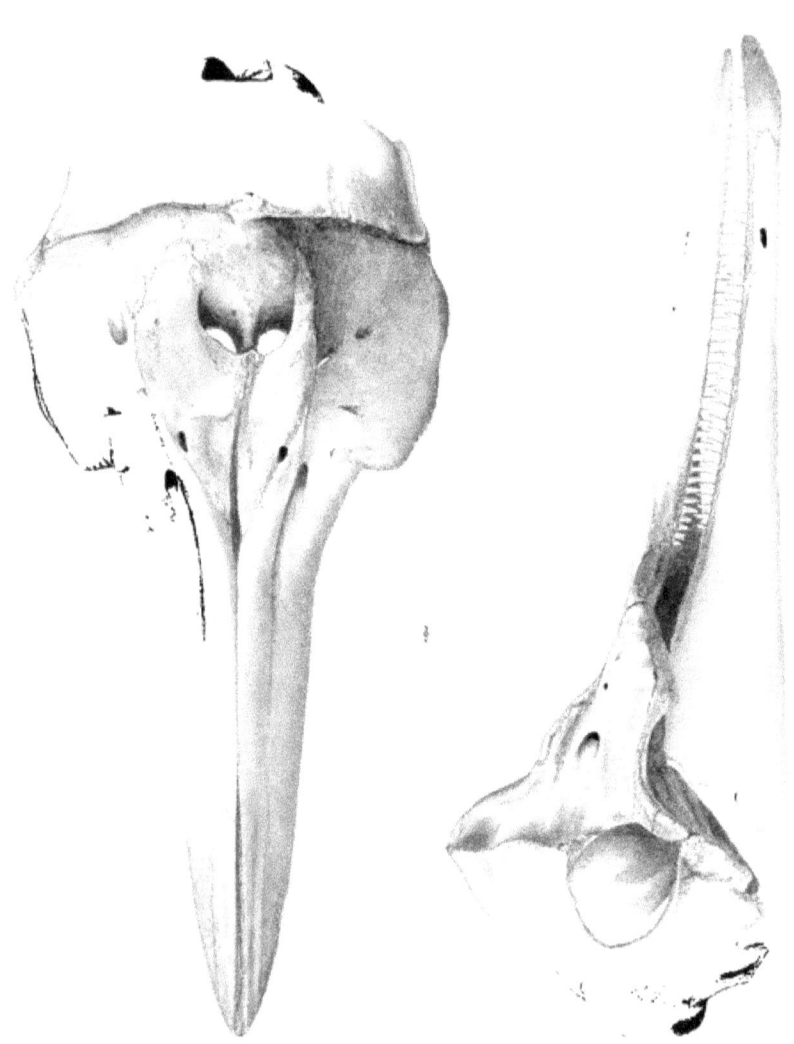

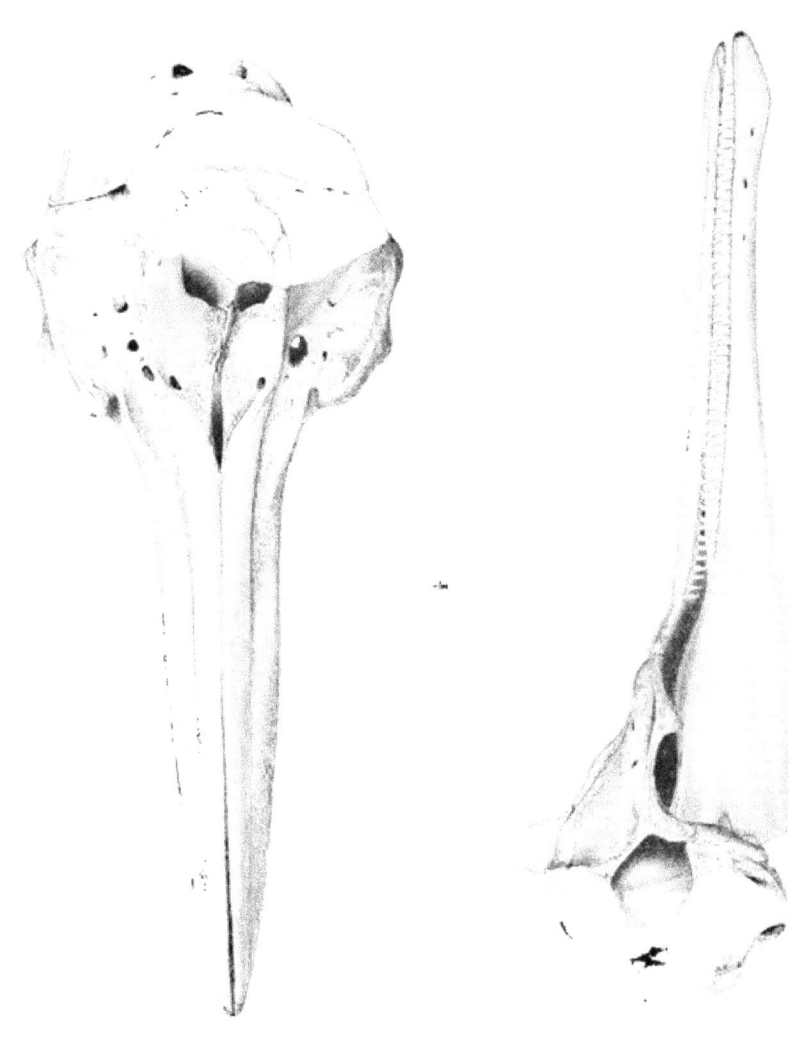

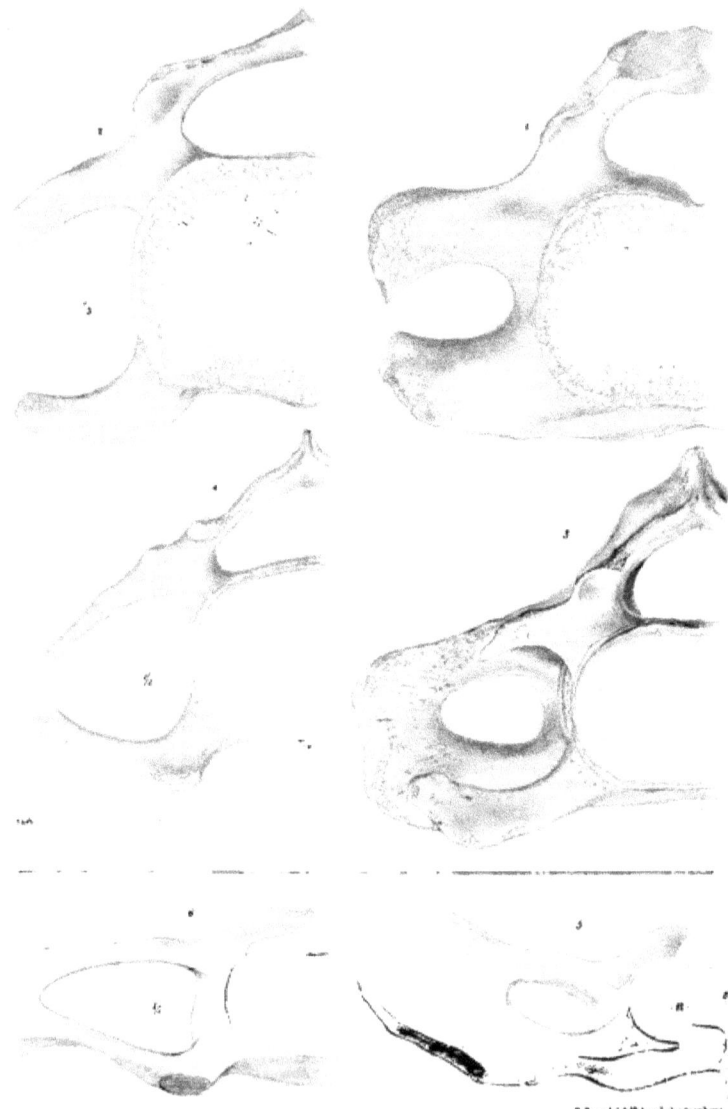

1 2 & 6 CERVICAL VERTEBRA OF BALÆNOPTERA (PERQUALUS) BOOPS
3 4 .... BALÆNOPTERA ROSTRATA
5 6 .... BALÆNOPTERA PHYSALUS ANTIQUARUM

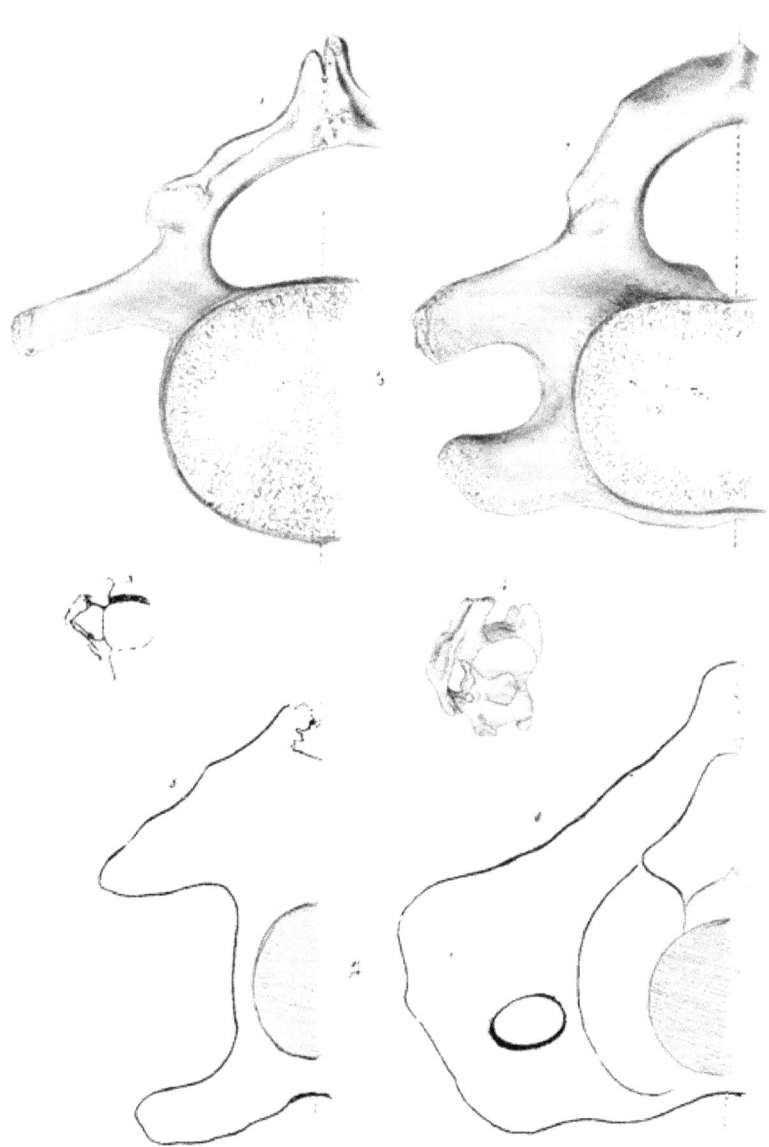

1, 2 MEGAPTERA LONGIMANA
3, 4   POESKOP (from Cuvier)
5, 6 BALÆNOPTERA (RORQUALUS) SIBBALDII

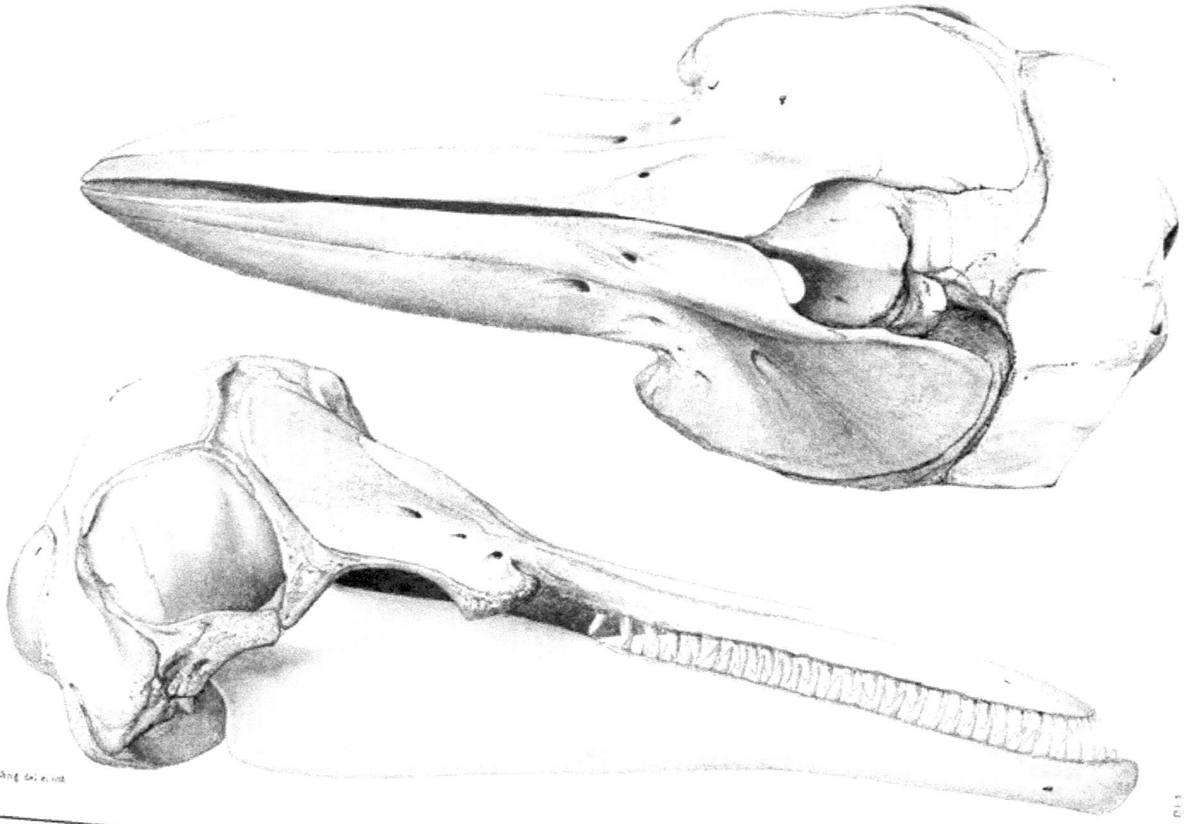

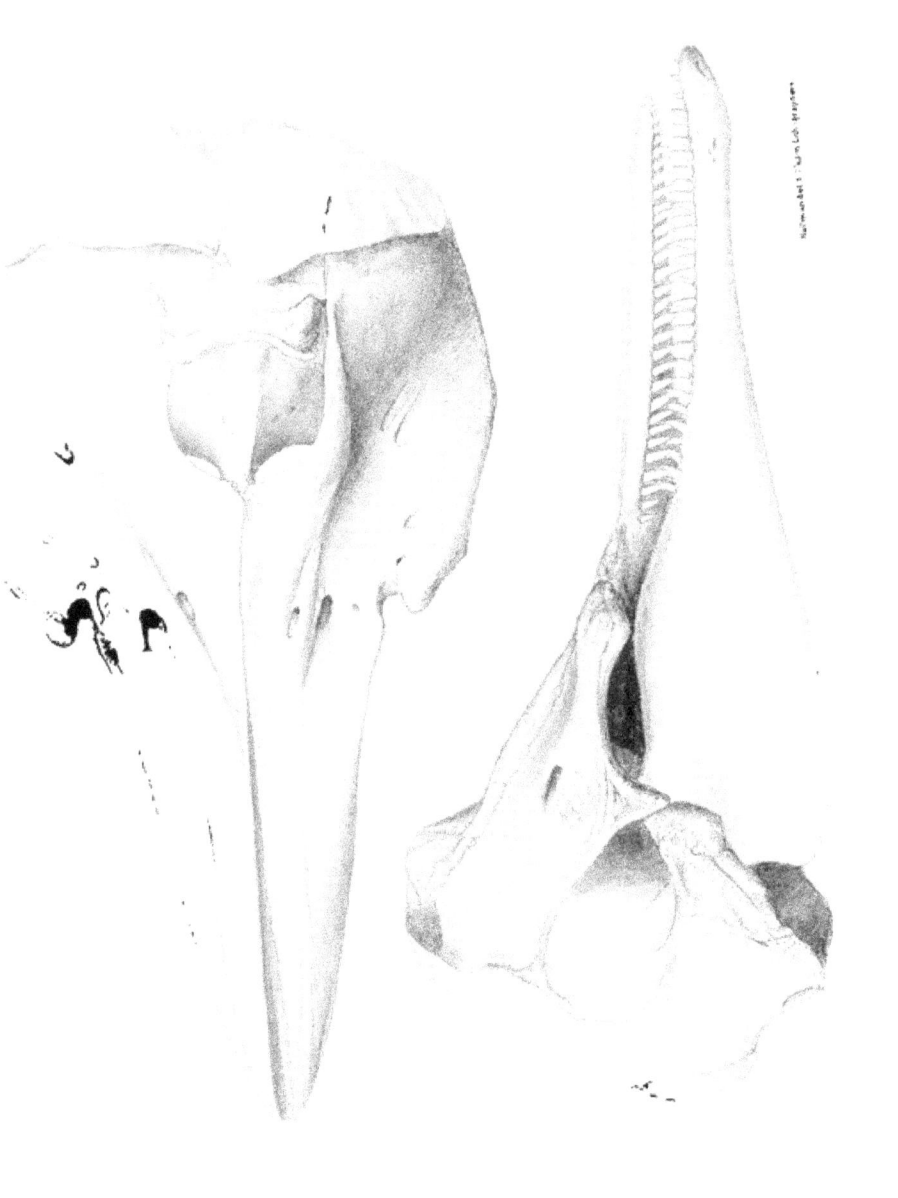

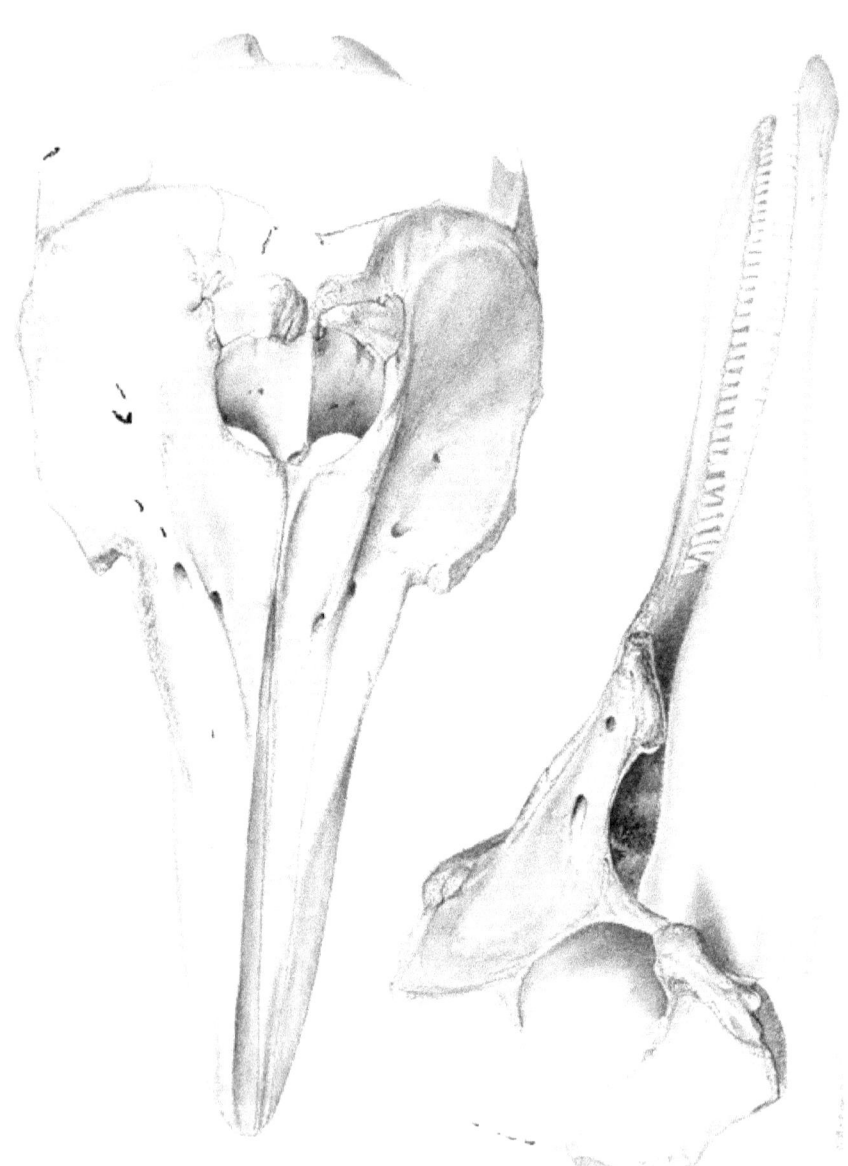

www.ingramcontent.com/pod-product-compliance
Lightning Source LLC
Chambersburg PA
CBHW020337090426
42735CB00009B/1577